WHAT PEOPLE ARE SAYING ABOUT

All Is Well

Valerie and her parents courageously tell a story of a prodigal's wandering and return. Their story breathes courage into the heart of every parent whose child is on a prodigal's journey. This prodigal's journey brought her home in answer to the faithful prayers of God's people and the persistent pursuits of the Holy Spirit.

Dr. John Neihof
President, Wesley Biblical Seminary

Be prepared to have your heart deeply stirred as Tim and Becky candidly share Valerie's incredible journey back home to Father's house. Valerie's personal reflections at the end of each chapter bring a special perspective to her own wonderful story of redemption. For every parent of a prodigal son or daughter, this is truly a must-read book that will challenge you to keep on praying, fasting, loving, and believing!

Mark Cravens
Senior Pastor at Kenwood Bible Methodist Church

This is a great book that will meet an enormous need for parents and grandparents. It is filled with practical wisdom and profound biblical principles. Most of all, it points people to Jesus and gives glory to God.

Troy Keaton
Lead Pastor at Eastlake Community Church

All Is Well reveals two perspectives of a prodigal's wandering and return: that of the wandering child and the wounded parents. Neither Tim, Becky, nor Valerie shy away from the painful elements of a dramatic story. Filled with heartfelt insight and thought-provoking challenges, this book is an encouragement to anyone confusing God's apparent silence with God's absence. The Keeps provide a powerful reminder that in a season of pain God may just be setting up the stage for the second act, one in which his faithfulness is on glorious display.

Keith Waggoner
Lead Pastor, Grace Bible Church

If your heart is heavy for a wayward child or grandchild, you must read this book! It is filled with powerful, redeeming truths from God's Word. The gripping accounts of God's grace in the midst of a parent's worst nightmare will bring you hope and inspire you to stay in the battle until God has won the victory.

Jeff Keaton
CEO & President, Renewanation

This book is a must-read. Through their own painful journey, Tim and Becky, with Valerie, have written a very honest and compelling book on the redemption of a prodigal. *All Is Well* is full of biblical insights gained through this real-life story; insights which are sure to strengthen, encourage, and challenge every parent and grandparent whose hearts are breaking over a wayward son or daughter.

Dr. Mark Smith
President, Columbia International University

All Is Well

Finding the Great Heart of God
When a Child Walks Away

All Is Well

Finding the Great Heart of God
When a Child Walks Away

Tim and
Becky Keep
with
Valerie Keep Jenkins

Copyright © 2019 by Tim and Becky Keep

ISBN: 978-1-948362-20-7

Published by Whispering Pines Publishing, Shoals, Indiana.

All rights reserved. No portion of this book may be reproduced, stored in a retrieval system, or transmitted in any form or by any means–electronic, mechanical, photocopy, recording, scanning, or other–except for brief quotations in critical reviews or articles, without prior written permission of the publisher.

All Scripture quotations, unless otherwise indicated, are taken from the NEW KING JAMES VERSION®. Copyright © 1982 by Thomas Nelson, Inc. All rights reserved.

Printed in Shoals, Indiana, by Country Pines Printing, Inc.

Jacket design by Shane Muir Graphic Design.

Printed in the United States of America

*In grateful praise
We prayerfully dedicate this grace story
To the parents and grandparents
Of prodigal children and grandchildren.*

CONTENTS

    Foreword 11

    Introduction 15

1. How Did We Get Here? 17

2. Sometimes it Takes a Struggle 23

3. A Mother's Worst Day 35

4. Check Your Motives 45

5. Don't Bury Your Prodigal 55

6. The Power of Unconditional Love 61

7. The Waiting 75

8. Praying *For* and *Against* the Prodigal 83

9. The Grace of Christian Community 93

10. He Must Win the Battle............................. 101

    Afterword 113

FOREWORD

In 2009 the Lord clearly led our family back to the USA after thirteen years of ministry in the Philippine Islands. Valerie, our eldest, was ready for college and Timothy, our eldest son, was a sophomore in high school. The Lord had provided for Jesse's (our third child, who is blind) educational needs for eight years in the Philippines, but Becky and I both felt it was time to tap into state side technology and resources for the blind and to prepare Jesse for independence. Carolyn and Samantha were still very young, so it was our older children's changing needs we needed to focus on. We had no idea how tough re-entry would be for our family, and how the Lord would use another season of turbulence to teach us more about his unconditional love.

By far, the greatest challenge we faced upon returning to the United States had to do with Valerie. Her painful spiritual and emotional struggle caused Becky and me to endure a season of grief like none we had yet endured. We felt helpless. We questioned ourselves and sometimes wondered aloud if our obedience to the missionary call had been worth it! There were moments when we *felt* abandoned by God and questioned his love and grace. We questioned his promises. In our darkest hour we were *tempted* by thoughts of betrayal, *feeling* that our obedience to God's call should have spared us this family pain. We wondered many days if he still heard and answered prayer. But grace held onto us in our brokenness! In this book we want to share part of this journey with you, especially those of you who can identify with our story.

ALL IS WELL

By the amazing grace of God we're on the other side of this struggle now. Today, Valerie is following Jesus, is married to a God-honoring man, Brent Jenkins, and they have given us two beautiful granddaughters, with one baby still in the "oven"! I'm pretty sure it's a boy!

Becky and I promised the Lord that if he would redeem our girl and make our family whole again we would never cease to praise him. Through these trials the Lord has taught us that while the Christian life will not spare us *sorrows,* it will provide us a perfect and beautiful *Savior,* one who will not fail to redeem our brokenness for his glory and redemptive purpose.

A few things you should know right up front:

1. This book has taken us a long time to write because we wanted Valerie to be ready … and willing. We're so thankful for her willingness to share her reflections in this story.

2. As with our other books, we have written it, *first*, as a record of God's faithfulness *to* our family, *for* our family. But if you, or a family you love, find yourself in circumstances similar to those you will read about in this book, we have written this for you as well.

3. We have written it because of the many prodigal stories we've heard, and we want to encourage other families to never give up hope!

4. We acknowledge that Valerie's season of waywardness may well be due *in part* to "MK" (missionary kid) re-entry trauma, and we accept our responsibility for not handling this as well as we should have. We just didn't know, and have asked Valerie to forgive us. But the passing of time and much reflection has made us even more confident that the root of her struggle was spiritual. Once her broken rela-

FOREWORD

tionship with God was healed, his healing grace began to flow to other areas of her life as well.

It is our prayer that he will pour out upon you greater and greater measures of his amazing grace in your family, as he has in ours, and that this story will be a part of that grace. –Tim

INTRODUCTION

One of the joys of summertime is the week that our daughter, Valerie, comes for a visit. She always brings the kids; and her husband, Brent, often comes with her if he can spare the time off work. It is a delightful week. My (Becky) mornings begin extra early as our little granddaughters wake up full of energy and ready to explore "Nana" and "Poppa's" back yard. I often nurse a cup of coffee while swinging pajama-clad little girls on the swing or drawing elaborate pictures on the back porch using sidewalk chalk. We spend long, hot days in the pool, applying and reapplying dollops of sunscreen to sweet baby skin. We sometimes pack a lunch and spend a day at the zoo, where the polar bears and hippos are a hit with the kiddos. And I mustn't forget our local ice cream stand, The Dairy Corner, which we patronize, usually more than once!

It was at the end of one such day that I walked into the living room to find Valerie sitting on the couch with both three-and-a-half-year-old Claire and one-and-a-half-year-old Macie. Both girls were bathed and ready for bed. Macie sat on Val's lap while Claire sat snuggled up under her left arm with her damp, freshly-shampooed head resting on her mommy's chest.

I settled down into my chair unnoticed while Valerie read from a Bible story book. The girls sat mesmerized as she read to them the story of Queen Esther and how she was used by God to save the Jewish people. I watched and listened, nearly overcome with emotion by the beauty of the scene playing out in front of me. I sat silently, my heart full and overflowing with gratitude to God for bringing all of us to this moment. I praised him for fulfilling the promise he had spoken to my heart so long ago during a season of praying for our prodigal girl that *"Someday the joy of her return will surpass the pain of her wandering."* I sat and basked in that joy.

It has been nearly a decade since the events that you will read in the coming chapters took place, but the wonder of the miracle has never waned. I pray that it never will! I worship the God who offers second chances—for both parents and children—for restoring what was shattered, and redeeming what had been lost, and for lavishing love and blessing beyond what we could have ever imagined on our family.

I would offer one caveat before you turn the page. As you read our story, please be mindful that much of it is meant to be *descriptive* rather than *prescriptive*. One of the dangers Tim and I are very aware of as we write is that some parents will compare their story with ours. The reality is that every child, every situation, and every answer to prayer is unique. But God is constant! On him we can always depend! –Becky

CHAPTER ONE

How Did We Get Here?

Not many days later, the younger son gathered all he had and took a journey into a far country, and there he squandered his property in reckless living.
Luke 15:13, ESV

I (Becky) laid face down on our couch in the darkened living room, unable to suppress the painful sobs that came from deep within me. Tim sat across the room in grief-laden silence. The unspoken question that hung heavily in the room was unanswerable. "How did this happen to us? How did we become *that* family?" It was unconscionable to both of us that only moments before, our teenage daughter, Valerie, had angrily walked out into the night, out of our home, and for the next nine months, out of our lives. The most difficult part for us was that it seemed she had also chosen to turn away from God. For months there had been strong undercurrents of resistance towards us and anyone who represented authority in her life. We had watched helplessly as one by one she discarded the principles and truths that we had so diligently instilled in her.

What followed were some of the most tumultuous days our family has known—days in which we searched desperately for answers—answers that would somehow make sense of what we were experiencing. Where had we gone wrong? Who was to blame? What must we change about our parenting? What must we do differently to ensure that our younger children wouldn't follow this same treacherous path? Were we even fit to parent? Did we veer from the "formula" of how to raise godly children? *Is* there a formula? *Our daughter's struggles must be evidence that we have failed miserably*, we thought.

I sat on Valerie's bed on the eve of her birthday, just two weeks after her departure. I gazed around the room at the bits and pieces of the things she'd left behind: the fun red and white decor that she'd always loved, framed pictures of her siblings, cousins, and friends, and the gifts scattered around the room that had been given to her upon leaving the land of her childhood just a few months before. With a heavy heart, I sat and allowed my mind to travel back to the day that she was born. I remembered feeling calm and prepared. I was in nursing school at the time and had just finished a three week rotation in OB at a nearby hospital. I had shared dozens of conversations with sisters and friends who had given birth. Tim and I had tuned in diligently to our childbirth training classes—watched the videos, read the books, and practiced our breathing techniques. Midway through the twenty-three hours of searing agony and intense work of bringing a baby into the world, however, it all felt useless. Head knowledge, the experiences of others, medical facts, coping methods, and even the promise of this new life grew dim in the excruciating fog of relentless pain.

Here I was, nearly twenty years later, shocked and overcome by pain which paralleled the pain of bringing her into the world. And in this place of mental agony nothing else mattered except that she break forth into spiritual life.

I realized that although pain with physical birth is expected, and even normal, we don't anticipate such piercing hurt when it comes to the spiritual birth of our children. After all, the Bible is full of promises that speak to the salvation of the children of the

HOW DID WE GET HERE?

righteous. Promises that bring hope and encouragement to parents. Promises that had kept us going through long years of child rearing—kept us training, teaching, loving, praying, and believing.

Can this really be happening? Can our daughter, who has always seemingly embraced the teachings of Scripture and professed Jesus as Savior at an early age, be so abruptly turning her back on the Lord?

Perhaps we were naive, but we had never entertained the possibility that Valerie would stray from the right path—the path of faith and obedience to Christ. This situation in which we found ourselves was opposed to all that we had anticipated.

I spent many hours writing out Scriptures and praying them aloud to my heavenly Father, often prefacing each one with, "Father, you promised in your Word that…."

> *The children of your servants will live in your presence; their descendants will be established before you (Psalms 102:28, NIV).*
>
> *The Lord's love is with those who fear him, and his righteousness with their children's children (Psalms 103:17a, NIV).*
>
> *"My Spirit, who is on you, and my words that I have put in your mouth will not depart from your mouth, or from the mouths of your children, or from the mouths of their descendants from this time on and forever," says the Lord (Isaiah 59:21, NIV).*

I prayed these Scriptures in desperation, and with many tears, wondering why the answer did not come sweeping in immediately. *I did not want to wait!* I wanted to employ all the "natural" methods at my disposal to somehow assist the God of the universe in fulfilling his promises. As if he needed my help.

As the dust of our broken hearts began to settle, and we realized that we were in this for the long haul, we began to seek the Lord in a deeper and more deliberate way than ever before. Through much trial and a lot of error we began to discern the heart of God as it related to our beautiful daughter.

ALL IS WELL

We learned to have hope even while realizing that God's promises don't always follow a straight line—that the path to answered prayer may take jagged, unexpected, and even unwanted turns. We understood that we were imperfect parents. We began to see that sometimes even when we've done our very best as parents, our kids have wills of their own and may make choices that delay the fulfillment of that promise. We identified with so many people in Scripture who also waited for God's promises to come to pass.

We learned that God always has a purpose in the wait. Ravi Zacharias once stated in a message that one of God's main purposes in allowing the children of Israel to wander in the desert for forty years was that they might see the true condition of their hearts. Perhaps it took this waiting for Valerie to see the true condition of her heart and the depth of her need. But it also took time for God to peel back some of the layers of pride in Tim and me and to reveal judgmental attitudes and certain misconceptions about godly parenting. This peeling away forced us to our knees in repentance and a more perfect reliance on him.

We learned that anger is counterproductive to winning the prodigal's heart. And we discovered with joy and absolute certainty that the *delay of God's promise doesn't equal the absence of his presence.*

Perhaps you are reading this and today your heart is breaking because of a wayward child, a grandchild, or a family member who seems to be hurtling down a dangerous path—a path that will surely end in destruction. You might be tempted to believe that your prayerful diligence in rearing children has been an exercise in futility. Or perhaps you know exactly the ways in which you have failed. Maybe today those things haunt you as they replay repeatedly in your mind. We hope our journey recorded in these few pages will encourage you.

Some parts of this book are a *description* of our journey—not necessarily a *prescription* for yours. The return of every prodigal

HOW DID WE GET HERE?

is unique. God has his own way, time, and plan for every life. The common denominator in our story and yours, however, is a loving heavenly Father who is all about bringing home the prodigal!

Our prayer is that your hope in God will be strengthened as you read this account—that your trust in the promises of God will be deepened and solidified. We pray that you will see that God is bigger and more powerful than both your failures and best efforts. We pray that you will be able to tune out the lies of Satan that torment you.

Most importantly, we want you to embrace the grace of God—to know that the salvation of your children, the preservation of their hearts, and the establishment of your home is all about grace. We want you to *lean* into that grace for the sake of that wayward child. And we want you to experience the very real peace and presence of God as you wait for the promise.

Valerie's Reflections

Valerie, when was the turning point when you said to yourself, "I'm leaving home!"? What could Mom and Dad have done to cause you to want to stay? How has your struggle shaped the person you are today?

I remember the night very clearly that I was confronted by my dad about a wrong choice I had made. That was the night I decided to pack my things and leave home. I have since discovered that I tend to be an all-or-nothing person. If I'm in, I'm 100% in, or not at all! Having been caught, once again, in this disobedience and sin, I felt that I had no other choice but to leave home, my school, and all my Christian friends, and to give way to my desires. I didn't want to live a double life anymore. I remember that night being very dramatic. I think what I needed more than the drama that night was to be talked off the ledge. I don't know if it would have worked. I don't know if I could have even been reasoned with at that point.

If you have a child or grandchild who, like me, is an "all-or-nothing" person who when stressed tends to run, I would say be calm. Sit your child down and explain to him/her that it is not the end of the world. They have not messed up their lives forever. They need to know that others have struggled in the same way—others have failed. Perhaps there are even failures in your life which God has graciously redeemed. Be vulnerable and share some of these stories.

I wish I could say that was the last time I tried to walk out on something or someone. God has had to deal with me about my tendency to want to get up and leave when times get tough. I am very thankful for a godly, anti-dramatic, loving husband who is willing to sit down and have those long, hard conversations in a loving way. I also thank God for giving me victory.

CHAPTER TWO

Sometimes it Takes a Struggle

*I have learned to kiss the wave that throws me against
the Rock of Ages.*
Charles Spurgeon

The first major crisis in Valerie's prodigal journey could hardly have been more devastating. She was in Bible college and I (Tim) was speaking that weekend in services about six hours from home.

My cell phone rang late in the afternoon just as I entered the sanctuary of the chapel for some moments of reflection and prayer. I recognized the voice of the college president on the other end of the line. He sounded sad but urgent. "Tim," he began, "I'm calling about Valerie. I'm so sorry to have to bring this news to you today.... She's been (in some trouble).... We're probably going to have to let her go. I'm calling a meeting of the discipline committee on Monday, and we'll need you and Becky to be here if possible. Tim, I'm so sorry...."

I couldn't believe what I was hearing! Our daughter expelled from a Christian college? Unthinkable! I knew she was struggling, but I never imagined it would come to this. I was crushed. I felt a grief so deep that only the parent of a prodigal can understand

ALL IS WELL

it. I didn't want to call Becky right away because I knew it would crush her, too. I called my mom, because I knew that she would stop whatever she was doing and pray for Valerie and for Becky and me. I couldn't hold back the tears as I shared the news, and she wept with me; but she also reminded me of how God had answered prayer for me so long ago. "He'll hear and answer our prayers for Valerie, just as he heard the prayers of your dad and me for you!" she said through her own tears. Her words brought a flood of memories into my mind.

I remembered the October evening in my senior year of high school when my rebellious, foolish choices began to catch up to me; when my self-centered sandcastles began to wash away in the tide of sin's consequences. I can still see myself on a cool evening looking up at the lighted window of the dean's office where decisions about my future in that institution were being discussed. I remember being told, without pleasure or malice, that I would have to pack my bags. I had broken the rules for the last time. I was being sent home.

I remember the difficult phone call I made to my parents. (I know now how hurt and angry they must have felt and how frightened they must have been by my sinful choices.) I remember the quiet seven-hour ride home. I remember the incredible mercy shown me by the administration in allowing me to return to the academy under *strict* probation! I remember how the consequences of sin captured my attention and began to soften my heart to the convicting voice of the Holy Spirit. Most of all, I remember the cold January night in 1987 that the Father drew me tenderly through the voice of a friend, met me on my knees at the front of the chapel, forgave my sins for Jesus' sake, and transformed my life by his amazing grace. The prayers of my family, friends, and teachers were finally answered. I who was blind, now saw. I who was dead, now lived. I who hated, now loved. I who desired the pleasures of sin suddenly wanted to do right. My life has never

SOMETIMES IT TAKES A STRUGGLE

been the same since that night. God's saving grace in my life was a fulfillment of 2 Corinthians 5:17: *"Therefore, if anyone is in Christ, he is a new creation. The old has passed away; behold, the new has come" (ESV)*. Mom was right: if God would go to such lengths to save this rebel, then surely he would do it for our daughter, too!

After the phone call with mom, I began to reflect on how God had prepared me all day long for the news about Valerie. It amazed me. It *still* amazes me! I had awakened early with a purpose. Sometime previous I had read a compelling passage on the life of the Old Testament character, Jacob, and I wanted to spend the day exploring its meaning. The passage I had read was from the book of Hosea:

> *He (Jacob) took his brother by the heel in the womb, and in his strength he **struggled** with God. Yes he **struggled** with the Angel **and prevailed**. He wept and sought favor from Him. He found Him in Bethel, and there He spoke to us.*[1]

It was Jacob's "struggle" that had captivated me! As I took a closer look at his life throughout the day I noted that *struggle* was a major theme in his life, but that through struggle and *surrender* God changed his name—his character.

- Jacob's struggles began in the womb,[2] which became a prophetic foreshadowing of Jacob and Esau's relationship and of the struggles between the nations they would father.
- Jacob struggled to gain his father's love. Jacob was a *momma's boy* while Esau was a *cowboy* favored by Isaac.[3] Don't think for a minute that this wasn't a painful wound in Jacob's heart.

---

1. Hosea 12:3-4, emphasis added
2. Genesis 25:22
3. Ibid. 27-28

ALL IS WELL

- Jacob's greatest struggle was with himself—his own flawed character and deceptive nature.[1] "Jacob" means "one who takes the heel; a deceiver." Grabbing the heel was symbolic of who Jacob was until God changed him. He was a man who constantly took advantage of others. He was an opportunist, shrewd, willing to tear others down to lift himself up.

- Because of Jacob's deceptive nature he struggled with relationships his entire life. Esau was called a *"profane man"*[2] because he sold his birthright for beans. But Jacob? Jacob was a self-centered brat! He took advantage of his brother in a moment of weakness[3] and even tricked his own father out of a blessing.[4] This deceptive act prompted Esau to exclaim, *"Is he not rightly named Jacob?"*[5] In other words, *"He's just like his name!"*

- Now Jacob would learn that living with the consequences of a self-centered life is no walk in the park. The deceiver is deceived! His father-in-law tricked him into marrying the "wrong" girl, his wages were changed ten times, his home was filled with sadness and conflict, and his life was controlled by fear and insecurity. Jacob's life was the fulfillment of Galatians 6:7: *"Be not deceived, God is not mocked. Whatever a man sows he shall also reap."*

That day as I continued to pour over this story, I saw Jacob's showdown with the Angel (likely Jesus) in a clearer light. The consequences of his deceptive life had caught up with him and he fi-

---

1. Ibid. 25:26
2. Hebrews 12:16
3. Genesis 25:31
4. Ibid., 27:1-29
5. Ibid., 27:36

nally realized how *desperately* he needed God. Esau was marching toward his family caravan with four hundred men and murder in his heart. Jacob had burned every bridge behind him and he couldn't turn around. His only hope was the favor of God—the God he had pushed aside all his life. God had Jacob hemmed in on all sides.

Jacob needed God, but God played hard to get! He resisted Jacob all night long. He even hurt him. Not because he's a cruel and angry God but because it took pain to humble this stubborn man and change his nature. Struggle was the chisel in the hand of the master Artisan, transforming Jacob's character.

Jacob's defining moment came when he became honest. It was that simple. His struggle wasn't as much with God as it was with himself. *"What is your name?"*[6] the Angel asked the exhausted wrestler. In other words, *"Who are you?"* And for the first time in Jacob's life he became completely honest. *"Jacob,"* he breathed. In other words, *"Yep, that's who I am! I'm the self-centered, deceitful opportunist who steps on anyone who dares to stand in my way. Even my own dad! Yes, I'm that guy!"* That's all God needed to hear. Without hesitation, without Jacob having to prove anything, without Jacob having to earn his favor, God gave the gift of grace: *"And He said, 'Your name shall no longer be called Jacob (heel-grabber), but Israel (Prince with God); for you have struggled with God and man and have prevailed.'… And He blessed him there.'"*[7]

Jacob's story is the story of grace! And that depressing, lonely afternoon, as I prayed alone in the chapel, I began to see Valerie's struggle in light of Jacob's; and I saw a ray of hope. *Perhaps God is letting Becky and me know*, I thought, *that this struggle of our daughter is God's wake-up call in her life—his way of exposing her sin and self-righteousness and forming her into a spiritual prin-*

---

6. Ibid., 32:27
7. Ibid., 27, 29

cess—a girl who prevails for God's blessing. "Please, God, let it be so," I prayed. Nearly a decade later we see this clearly, but up until this moment neither Becky nor I had entertained the thought that spiritual struggle might fit into God's plan for one of our kids.

Monday morning found Becky and me and Valerie in the president's office. Valerie was treated with kindness and was offered grace. Within her heart a battle was raging, and her countenance gave her away. She pushed the hand of grace aside, because grace wasn't what she wanted. Everyone in the room was stunned by her resistance. But this was only the beginning.

We could not have imagined how violent Valerie's struggle would become over the next weeks and months. She lashed out at those who loved her most. She kicked against every boundary. One painful night she piled her belongings on the curb and against the pleadings of her family drove off into the night, and for the next nine months she would be almost completely beyond our reach. It was all so unbelievable to Becky and me then, and especially now when we see the beautiful disciple of Jesus Valerie has become today.

Two Dangerous Mindsets

There was a dangerous "formula" that God had to purge from Becky and me, and he used Valerie's struggle to do it. The formula goes something like this: Godly parents, plus godly training, equals children who will not struggle spiritually. According to this formula, spiritual struggle is attributed to the failure of parents, which forms a toxic mix of shame and judgment. Satan uses this mindset to hurt parents, to wreck their faith, and to hinder their prayers. Parents can't pray as fervently and effectively when they believe their prodigal is a judgment for their parental unfaithfulness. One of the reasons we have written this book is to battle this mindset.

SOMETIMES IT TAKES A STRUGGLE

Until we traveled this road with Valerie, I think we assumed this formula was true. We read precious promises and *stood* on them—promises such as:

> Praise the Lord!
> Blessed is the man who fears the Lord,
> who greatly delights in His commandments!
> His offspring will be mighty in the land;
> *the generation of the upright will be blessed.*[1]

And,

> Train up a child in the way he should go;
> even when he is old he will not depart from it.[2]

Though we believe these promises today more than ever, we also believe that the fulfillment of God's promises to families is sometimes a bumpy ride. Between the training and the blessing some young people struggle—especially the more stubborn or self-righteous ones. It does not have to be this way, but for some it is. Before some young people will truly own the gospel for themselves, they *may* need to wrestle with God and themselves; and we need to let them, as painful as it may be.

Too often, well-meaning parents and grandparents rescue their prodigals from the discomforts—the struggles—God wants to use to change their character. When they do this, they enable prodigal behavior and thereby prolong the misery and wandering. Unwise intervention often hinders the Holy Spirit. As one of my former professors reminded me recently: *Had the Prodigal Son received care packages from his father's house, he may never have returned from the far country!* Hunger pains play an important role in the salvation of prodigals.

---

1. Psalm 112:1-2
2. Proverbs 22:6

ALL IS WELL

There is a second mindset that is just as destructive as the formula mindset: the mindset that raising godly kids is simply a *roll of the dice*! It's just luck! We've heard parents say things like, *"Hey, kids have a will of their own, so at the end of the day there's not really much we can do! It's their choice."* And while we agree that God has wonderfully created each child with a will of their own, sometimes these statements sound like indifference, as though parents are using their children's power of choice as an escape from the burden and responsibility of birthing godly children.[1] How grateful I am that when I was a wayward young man my parents didn't shrug their shoulders and let me go to hell, but trusted in the power of the Holy Spirit to convict me of sin. My mother prayed *my* "free will" under conviction! Years after my conversion I learned of the sleepless nights she spent "standing in the gap" for me.[2] It's no wonder that on a January night when I wasn't looking for God he came seeking me with such love and conviction that I found him irresistible.

Yes, there's plenty for Christian parents and grandparents to *do*, and we will be held accountable to God for our obedience. We *are* commanded to bring up children in the training and admonition of the Lord.[3] We *must* teach God's Word to them *diligently* and cultivate nurturing relationships out of which God conversations become a normal part of family life.[4] And parents must stand in the gap through fervent intercessory prayer.[5]

But the greatest danger of these good works is *trusting* the good works to save our kids. They can't. Salvation and character transformation is *always* a miracle of grace. Parents cultivate

---

1. Galatians 4:19
2. Psalm 106:23
3. Ephesians 6:4
4. Deuteronomy 6:7
5. Ephesians 6:18

SOMETIMES IT TAKES A STRUGGLE

the soil and plant the seeds, but only God can make them grow. We can even enforce certain behavior, but only God can open the blinded eyes of our kids. Only he can make them see.

So, the formation of godly character in our kids is neither a formula nor a roll of the dice. Beware of both extremes.

As I wrap up this chapter, I want to offer some final words of challenge and encouragement to parents and grandparents of prodigals:

First, learn to see the struggles of the prodigal as the hunger pains that will drive them to the Bread of Life, and as the pressure necessary for the forming of princely character! Let God teach you when to let them struggle and when to intervene.

Second, don't ever think that by moving the *biblically principled* "fences" your family has established you will save the prodigal. If your family fences—rules for worship, relationships, technology, lifestyle, etc.—have been built with love and are biblical and reasonable, then moving them will not save your son or daughter. Good fences unwisely moved will only have to be moved again ... and again.

This counsel was given to Becky and me by an older pastor and his wife whom we deeply respect and who had fought (and won) the same battle we were fighting. And we are forever grateful to them for their wisdom.

Be sure, however, that your rules are biblical and principled. Young people can see straight through hypocrisy and legalistic rules only meant to impress your religious tradition.

Third, never give up hope. Meditate on God's promises until faith rises within you. Don't let Satan tell you that God won't help your prodigal because of the mess *they've* made or mistakes *you've* made. The only people God can't help are the proud: *"God resists the proud but gives grace to the humble."*[6]

---

6. James 4:6

ALL IS WELL

Fourth, stand in the gap through prayer. God said that he would have destroyed the young nation of Israel had not Moses stood in the gap. Like Moses, pray promises of God and refuse to give up. This kind of intercession is a mighty force.[1]

Fifth, don't judge families who struggle, not even in your heart. Pray for them and be a source of comfort and encouragement.

Sixth, remember that the end of spiritual struggle doesn't mark the end of life's pain and problems—or even big mistakes. Not in Jacob's life! Not in the life of the prodigal!

---

1. Ibid., 5:16

Valerie's Reflections

What impact do you think being an "MK" had on you as you returned to American life? And what are some things you think Mom and Dad should have been aware of that would have helped you with the transition?

The days leading up to coming back to the US for college were exciting for me. The thought of being around family and friends back home was thrilling. I was caught up in thinking about all the new and fun things that were ahead and could not have realized just how dramatic the change would be. Life was so fast paced in America compared to our slower, simpler way of living in the Philippines.

When we arrived home, it immediately dawned on me that I was way behind. My friends and cousins had jobs, driver's licenses, cars, and some even had boyfriends. I remember voicing my concerns to my parents. I was craving some independence and wanted to "catch up" with the rest of the world as soon as possible.

My dad sat me down one day and told me there was no need to rush, to slow down and enjoy college life, and that the other things would come together with time. Ten years later I understand where he was coming from (why was I in such a hurry again?). I know that our entire family was in transition. We were temporarily staying with family while waiting to close on our "new" home. I felt that my parents didn't understand my perspective and my desire to feel like a "normal" eighteen-year-old American girl. This was their first time to experience this as well!

We didn't know that there were re-entry programs for MKs. I think that would have been a great option for me. I would say to other missionary kids who are re-entering their homeland: Don't be afraid to communicate your needs and fears to your parents, and parents be quick to listen and understand.

I realize, however, that some of these things were only catalysts that brought the real needs in my heart to the surface. It was painful for both me and my family, but I praise God for his grace in all our lives.

CHAPTER THREE

A Mother's Worst Day

It's our responsibility to do the possible, it's God's responsibility to do the impossible. The "possible" includes physical care for our children, teaching, training, pointing them to Christ. The "impossible" lies in the realm of miracles—conviction of sin, hunger and thirst for righteousness, and conversion. We are incapable of these, so there is rest in leaving the impossible up to God.
Ruth Bell Graham

I (Becky) won't forget the day that, while on my knees mopping a dirty kitchen floor, I paused to listen to the words of a song playing over the radio. "It is well, it is well, there is peace in my despair, knowing God will hear my prayer...."[1] *"Peace in my despair"?* I had plenty of despair, but truthfully, very little peace. I was barely surviving each day. I was scarcely sleeping at night. I was muddling through my waking hours and through my responsibilities as a wife and mom either woodenly or emotionally distraught. My brain was riddled with constant worry over the whereabouts and condition of our daughter.

---

1. "Elisha's Song," original song by The Isaacs from the album "Eye of the Storm"

ALL IS WELL

This song was a simple retelling of the story from 2 Kings, chapter four. It recounts the story of the Shunammite woman whose son died suddenly but was resurrected by the power of God through the prophet Elisha. I sat back and let the words penetrate my mind.

I knew this story. I had read it many times but had never contemplated this mother's powerful words when faced with an unthinkable tragedy. I left my mop water and settled down with my Bible and notebook to take a closer look. I began to read slowly through this story and became captivated with the events that took place in the life of a very ordinary woman.

I read that one day her son became ill while in the field with his father. He came home complaining of a headache. And after several hours of holding him on her lap, this young boy suddenly died. It's hard to imagine what must have taken place in her mind in that moment, but we do know the action she took. She carried her precious son to the prophet's bed and leaving him there set out to visit the prophet!

She asked her husband for permission to saddle the horses; and when he asked about her hurry, she said simply, "All is well!"[1] This statement shocked me! *All is well? What? How could anything be well in that moment? The reality was that her son of promise lay lifeless on the prophet's bed! This mother would soon be planning a funeral!* I read on. The Shunammite woman was on a mission. She hurried to find the prophet, even instructing her servant to drive the horses speedily in order to reach Elisha quickly.

Elisha spotted her from a distance. He could see that she was in a hurry. His concern for her caused him to send his servant running to see if there was a problem. I pictured in my mind Gehazi running to meet the Shunammite mother. I can hear his breathless inquiry: *"Are you ok? Is it well with you? With your husband? With*

---

1. 2 Kings 4:23

A MOTHER'S WORST DAY

your child?" Her response, again, made no sense to me. There were those same words once again, *"All is well." What? Is she delusional? Things certainly were not well,* I thought. *She should be falling apart! Her boy ... her promise from God just died in her arms!*

Suddenly, I had to know for myself just how this mother had been able to say those words, "All is well," on what was undoubtedly the worst day of her life.

I continued my search, delving into this passage, rereading this story and meditating on each verse and event. I sensed that God had something to say to me—a message that he wanted me to hear and internalize. As the Holy Spirit illuminated his Word, I began to see the source of power and confidence in this woman's life. I saw how it had enabled her to believe God even when facing the unthinkable. As I read on, the tears flowed and hope began to rise in my heart.

As I read slowly through the passage I discovered some amazing things about the Shunammite mother:

First, before she was a mother, she had been a woman who gave God a prominent place in her life and home.

The town where she lived was a destination often traveled by the prophet Elisha. She was aware of this and invited him to join her and her husband for a meal. She was very persuasive, and even insistent, that he be refreshed and fed in her home. And she didn't stop with an occasional meal, but asked her husband to build a small chamber where the prophet could spend the night whenever he passed through their town. They prepared Elisha's own personal hotel room, always ready when he needed to rest, write, or spend time in contemplation or prayer. *Here was a woman who was convinced that time in the presence of the man of God was valuable,* I thought, *and she found it no inconvenience to give of her time and money to care for him.*

I allowed my imagination to wander... I thought of the many nights, perhaps, that the Shunammite and her husband had lingered over a late dinner by firelight listening to the prophet tell of the mighty power of God. How thrilling it must have been to have heard the firsthand account of Elisha's traveling days with the prophet Elijah; of the day when Elisha witnessed Elijah's journey to heaven in a chariot; of the double portion of the spirit of Elijah that he received; of the parting of the waters when Elisha struck them with Elijah's mantle; of the healing of the waters of Jericho; of the miracle of the widow whose jar of oil never ran dry.

Did these, and countless other stories, come rushing back to the Shunammite's memory on the morning her son died? I wondered. Without a doubt! Was she reminded of the presence of God that she and her husband had experienced in their home through the anointing resting on this man of God? Surely the needs of her son could be met by this same God through his prophet! No wonder this mother could believe all was well even when the pain in her heart told her it wasn't!

If we want the faith of the Shunammite—faith for the resurrection of our children—we must make God preeminent in our lives. How imperative it is for our hearts to be permeated with the presence of God. His Word must have a prominent place in everything we do and every decision we make. Before we are parents or grandparents we must first be lovers of God.. Only then, when the troubles of life come crashing in around us, can we look those troubles in the face and say: *"All. Is. Well!"* And we can say it from the *depth* of our being, *knowing* that the God whom we know intimately has the power to deliver us in our time of need.

Parents cannot afford to have a "casual" relationship with God. If we want to see our prodigals return to the Father, we must get serious about placing God first in our own lives.

A second reason for the Shunammite's confidence was that she was what the Bible called a *"great"* woman. In my studies I learned that the term *"great"* implies that she was not only a

A MOTHER'S WORST DAY

wealthy woman, but a woman who *feared sin*.[1] This was what made her great!

When the moment of crisis came, and the life of her little boy was snuffed out, she could say "All is well" with no hindrance to faith, because she feared sin, and because there was nothing between her and God. There was no uncertainty in her heart, because she enjoyed a right standing before God. There was no guilty conscience to chip away at her belief that God would indeed resurrect her boy.

I would like to submit to every parent reading this today that we must be people who fear sin! If we would trust God for the spiritual life of our kids we cannot take the matter of sin lightly in our own lives. Do not misunderstand me. Personal godliness will never save our kids. Only God can save, and his salvation is always a work of grace. But *obedience cultivates faith*, and God's saving grace is poured out in the life of our children as an answer to our prayers of faith[2]. Do not underestimate the devastating effect of harboring unconfessed sin. If there is something God has clearly placed his finger upon in your life, your obedience will strengthen faith and enable you to believe God for the salvation of your child. Again, o*bedience cultivates faith!*

As God opened this truth to me that morning, I wept and asked him to search my heart and bring to light sins in my life I needed to confess. He was so faithful and did just that. As I confessed, my faith was restored; and I was able to pray with fresh fervor and clarity for our daughter.

A third powerful truth gripped my heart as I lingered over the Shunammite mother's story. **I realized that when her son died in her arms, she chose the supernatural response over the natural.**

---

1. Adam Clarke, Commentary on 2 Kings 4:8, "A woman eminent for piety before God; a woman fearing sin"

2. James 5:17

ALL IS WELL

She never, even for a moment, acted as though her child's life was up to her.

She did not try to revive him by her own wisdom. She didn't perform CPR, call the doctor, or try to waken him. She made preparations and went straight to the one whom she *knew* had the power to resurrect her son! This mother instinctively knew that this was not *"her moment"!* This was a *"divine moment"!* This was not *her battle*! This was *God's battle*!

As I thought about this, the Holy Spirit gently revealed to me how often, over the past weeks, I had made this battle for Valerie's soul my own battle. I realized that I had been living and acting as if I had the power to save my child. I would not have said out loud, "Our daughter's spiritual life is up to Tim and me," but I believe that, like so many other well-meaning Christian parents, we had given ourselves much more capital in the salvation of our kids than we actually owned.

I realized that morning that in the face of my daughter's spiritual struggle I was guilty—with my words, my tears, my pleading, and my pouting—of trying to produce spiritual life in her through my own efforts. I was acting as if her spiritual day of resurrection was up to me. *Perhaps if I can just say one more word, tell her one more thing, warn her of one more dire consequence, show her how unhappy this makes me, then I might be able to compel her to repent and turn back to the Lord!*

Please don't misunderstand me. I believe in parental intervention. I know that diligently training our children is the most important task we will ever be entrusted with. But the truth that was hammered into my consciousness that morning was that, *at the end of the day, none of my efforts, no matter how good and well intentioned, have the power to bring spiritual life to my child*. I realized that my daughter was spiritually "dead," not because of a lack of knowledge, but because she had chosen to turn away from that knowledge to embrace a lie. And I understood that because she was dead, all my tactics were falling upon deaf ears and blind eyes! How freeing it was to direct all my petitions to the God who is all about life! I could indeed turn my anxious heart to him knowing that he could breathe warmth and life into what was cold and dead.

I thought about how we parents can sometimes make kids conform and make them *appear* well for a while, but only divine transformation will make them truly well. The only one who possesses the power to transform your child and mine is God Almighty through the power of his Holy Spirit.

That morning my mind was reawakened to my utter dependence on the Lord to do his work in her heart. I had done my part. I could trust him to do what I was powerless to accomplish. With the fresh glimpse of his absolute authority came peace, and I was truly able to relinquish Valerie to him.

To you, my friend, perhaps you are reading this and identify with the miserable, hopeless, anxious "me" depicted in the first paragraph of this chapter. Maybe your child appears to you to be beyond the hope of redemption.

Perhaps you need to reevaluate your relationship with God. Is he first in your life?

Are you in the Word, allowing it to shape your thoughts, desires, and actions?

Are you a person who fears sin?

Do you find yourself scheming and endeavoring to bring about change in the life of your loved one using fleshly weapons? Do you over speak, manipulate, plead, pout, and expend all of your energy trying to bring about your own miracle?

I implore you to focus your hope for resurrection fully on Jesus! Read his Word. Internalize it. Believe it. Allow it to become the foundation of your life. Confess any sin that is hindering you, no matter how small it may be. Refuse to use the futile means of the flesh, and lean into the power of God. Relinquish your loved one up to him, knowing that he is *"not willing that any should per-*

ALL IS WELL

ish but that all should come to repentance."[1] *Knowing* that the *"any"* and *"all"* includes *your* prodigal!

In a subsequent chapter I will share one more powerful lesson that I learned from this Shunammite's most unlikely response to the death of her son.

---

1. 2 Peter 3:9

Valerie's Reflections

What were some of the most formative influences in your life as a child, and then as a teenager? Do you ever remember a time not wanting to serve the Lord? Were there negative influences which pulled you away from the Lord?

Without a doubt, my parents were the most formative influences in my life. There were times during my teen years that I didn't necessarily "like" them, but I always knew that they were the real deal. I never saw a trace of hypocrisy in my parents, and I knew they had my best interest at heart. Even in the height of my rebellion, I knew in my heart that their advice and pleading came from a place of truth. And I can honestly say that throughout my time of struggling, the desire for the God they knew and lived and taught was never gone. I wanted to do my own thing, but I knew that I would never have the life that I really wanted if I didn't surrender to God.

I lived a very sheltered life in the Philippines and was not aware of many things that American teenagers are exposed to. Coming home to the US and jumping right into college and dorm life was overwhelming. I learned many "things" very quickly, and because of my desire to fit in I allowed the wrong things to take root in my heart. This led me down a prodigal path for a season.

CHAPTER 4

Check Your Motives

The pain over a wayward child is real, and ought to be present in a life driven by the Spirit. Jesus wept over Jerusalem....

This pain shouldn't be confused, though, with our carnal desire to display to the world around us what "blessed" and "successful" families we have. In many cases, the real tragedy in a family with rebellious children isn't that their parents hurt for them, but that their parents are embarrassed of them. If "good" children were the result of mere technique, then we could boast of our own righteousness through the lives of our children. They're not.
Russell Moore[1]

Embarrassment is a very real temptation when a child fails to live up to our expectations.

We had returned to the USA after nearly thirteen years of serving as missionaries to the Philippine Islands. Our children had always been an integral part of our ministry. They had grown up hiking the mountains with us as we ministered in churches and

---

1. Russell Moore, *Love Your Prodigal As Yourself,* www.thegospelcoalition.org

villages, bringing the gospel and physical healing to many through evangelism, teaching, and medical relief.

Valerie was a typical firstborn. She had thrived from the age of three at helping me (Becky) with every aspect of housework, child care, and even cooking. Her favorite pastime as a preschooler was hauling her life-size baby doll, "Jonathon," everywhere she went. He was nearly as big as she, and it was so cute to watch her "mother" this very real looking baby. She transferred all of this maternal love to her brother, Timothy, the moment he came home from the hospital. I nearly fainted the day that I caught three-and-a-half-year-old Valerie half carrying, half dragging a clueless Tim Jr. across the room!

Valerie was kind of an "old soul." She took life and every task that she was given very seriously. Her little brothers and sisters knew better than to argue when she was in charge. It makes us smile even today to think of how she used to "whip" the younger kids in and out of the shower, cleaning them up, combing their hair, and making sure they looked great! Jesse especially hated this routine as a toddler and *endured* it, usually wearing a storm cloud on his face. Whether it was school work, housework, or any other responsibility, Valerie was an efficient "get-it-done" kind of kid. It was impressive to say the least. I always joked that Valerie could work circles around me. It was true! Sometimes we teasingly called her "Cinderella" because she loved to clean. Once, after she had become overly impatient with the boys for tracking dirt on the floors, Tim disciplined her by grounding her from mopping the floors for a week! It's humorous now, but back then ... not so much.

I don't remember ever having to tell Valerie to do her schoolwork. It was normal for her to set an alarm, get right up, and start working by 6:30 a.m. She'd finish up by 10:00 a.m. and have the remainder of the day free from school. This baffled me, as I had been a consummate procrastinator as a child. I remember asking myself how in the world I ever ended up with a kid like her.

CHECK YOUR MOTIVES

Valerie and I were also a seamless duo when it came to preparing our house for mission teams. I depended on her for so much. By the age of fourteen she could have run the house as competently as any grown woman.

Valerie was also actively involved with the students of our Bible college. She was often invited to participate with them in ministry opportunities. Singing, conducting Bible studies for children, and teaching Sunday school were just a few of the things she was involved in.

It wasn't until our last two years on the field that we sensed some growing discontent in her. We prayed a lot and had many conversations with her about her life goals. We did our best to be understanding. It had to be difficult being sixteen years old, so far away from cousins, friends, and the opportunities of American life. She felt that perhaps she was "missing out." Tim and I carried a real burden for her during these days. Tim remembers his early morning prayer walks for her, and some late evening conversations with her in her room. As she cried, he cried! *"Valerie, if somehow I could take all this pain away from you I would,"* he said. *"But I promise you that as soon as the Lord will release us from ministry here, we will take you 'home' and help you get settled in the life-path God has chosen for you."* And he kept this promise by asking our board to let us use the final year of our three year term as a transition year. They agreed, and we're very grateful for their understanding.

And so here we were, back in the US just in time for Valerie to enroll in college. It was an exciting time for all of us. Resettling back in our home country after being away for so long was also both scary and invigorating.

After only four months, the life of our beautiful firstborn began to unravel before our very eyes. We watched in horrified disbelief as this responsible, respectful, efficient, intelligent girl made decisions with little or no thought of the consequences.

ALL IS WELL

We struggled to keep our heads above the tsunami of emotions that followed. Anger—*how could she be acting so irresponsibly? She knows better!* Fear—*how are her actions and lack of regard for what is right going to permanently alter her life?* Disbelief—*this has to be a bad dream. Our daughter can't be making these choices!* But perhaps the most difficult of all, humiliation—*what are people—our family, friends, and supporters going to think about us? What kind of parents have we been? We must have been dreadfully incompetent, and now the whole world will know what failures we've been!*

We loved Valerie so fiercely, and she had always made us proud. She'd always done the "right" thing and acted responsibly. It had always made us feel pleased when others around us saw these wonderful attributes in her as well. And I'm sure we are not different than most other parents.

When our kids thrive, and our friends and peers take notice, it does seem to reflect well on us. It makes us look good. When our kids do well we tend to applaud ourselves for a *job well done*! And we hear the applause of others, too.

On the other hand, when they stumble, make mistakes, disappoint us, and are bent on destroying themselves and others, it also reflects poorly on us. Sadly, until our struggle with Valerie, I had been guilty of looking at parents whose children were struggling and had secretly wondered, *"What have they done wrong?"* Tim and I have had to repent of this graceless spirit of judgment. We've confessed it as sin. Jesus' command could not be clearer: *"Judge not, that you be not judged. For with the judgment you pronounce you will be judged, and with the measure you use it will be measured to you."*[1] It's one thing to make biblical evaluations based on facts, but it is another thing altogether to assume things we don't know. This un-Christlike rush to judgment creates a lot of pain in the body of Christ and makes hurting families feel isolated and alone.

---

1. Matthew 7:1-2 (ESV)

CHECK YOUR MOTIVES

It was painful to feel the burning sting of judgment. Some of this pain was self-inflicted. We assumed that certain people were condemning us when they were not. There were Bible teachers we avoided because we had heard their teaching and feared their counsel would only make us feel worse. And I was ashamed to discover that while we longed for Valerie's spiritual restoration, I was suffering way too much embarrassment. I was far too concerned with how Valerie's sin was making Valerie's parents look, and how she was sullying our reputation. I remember the day when God whispered in my heart, *"Becky, this is not about you and Tim. This is not about what people think of you, your ministry, your life as missionaries, or your parenting. This is only about the eternal destiny of your daughter."*

Pride in parents can delay the prodigal's return. That sentence may be one of the most important sentences in this book! I hope you will think about it. We have noticed that one of the greatest hindrances to the spiritual restoration of a wayward child is the pride of their parents.

While writing this story, I (Tim) was speaking in another country when a woman approached me and desired that I pray for the salvation of her daughter. This very young girl had made a terrible "mistake," one which had brought pain and humiliation to the entire family, especially her parents. Though unmarried she had become pregnant. And in an attempt to "protect" themselves from great embarrassment and from the judgments of their local Christian community, these parents kept their daughter out of sight and isolated. Because they feared what people would think and say, they kept her hidden. I made it clear that I felt this response to a daughter's sin, while perhaps quite natural in their context, was exactly the wrong response. And I pleaded with this broken-hearted mother to consider a more wise, biblical approach.

"If you really want to see your daughter fully restored," I said, "you must never allow shame to guide your responses. Remember that our Lord Jesus hung naked on a cross and suffered a most humiliating death, not because *he* had done wrong, but because *we* had. Because of his unconditional love, he willingly took our sin, and the shame of it, upon himself. And while he hung suspended between heaven and earth, most of the people who gathered around the cross, and those who passed by the cross, mocked him and scoffed his name. But because of Jesus' humility he was raised to life three days later by the power of the Holy Spirit. Humility led to grace!"

> *But he gives more grace. Therefore it says, "God opposes the proud but gives grace to the humble" (James 4:6, ESV).*

"But you don't realize how difficult this is in our culture," this lady said. "People will talk!" "I *do* understand," I said. "It happens in America, too. But in any culture the act of covering or hiding sin will only drive us and those we love further into bondage, while confession and repentance will lead to forgiveness and restoration. The path to healing and restoration for prodigals and their parents is the low road of humility, because God will never turn away from the broken, contrite heart. Pride—the attempt to protect one's reputation through false pretenses—will result in God's resistance, feed suspicion, fuel gossip, and prolong misery, while reaching out in honesty to our Christian community will open the floodgates of grace, silence rumors, increase prayer support, and hasten recovery."

> *Whoever conceals his transgressions will not prosper, but he who confesses and forsakes them will obtain mercy (Proverbs 28:13, ESV).*

I went on to explain to my friend that if I were in her position today, I would make sure my daughter knew that I loved her unconditionally, and walk proudly beside her through the process

CHECK YOUR MOTIVES

of repentance, forgiveness, and restoration. "If you will do this," I urged, "you can more fully entrust your daughter's spiritual restoration to God."

I (Becky) knew that I had to lay aside my pride and cry out to God for forgiveness—forgiveness for my judgmental attitude and for my fear of man. Fear, according to God's Word, always brings a snare. I needed to lift my countenance to heaven and intercede for Valerie without any motivation other than her redemption.

I had to believe God more than what I saw in Valerie and in myself. I had to trust that despite any parental shortcomings (yes, there were undoubtedly many), God would still hear and answer our prayer. And I had to refrain from the temptation to nuance our daughter's choices in a way that minimized our part, or that excused, explained away, or glossed over Valerie's wrong choices. I began to see these as self-preserving tactics intended to soothe my pride, but in the end would hinder the outpouring of God's grace. My perspective began to change as I allowed God to show me my heart. I wanted his pleasure and friendship because I knew that without his gracious leadership we really had no way through the fog and the pain.

We parents are often the key to the return of the prodigal child. And God often breaks the stronghold in *us* before he breaks it in our children. Perhaps as you have read this chapter the Holy Spirit has identified some areas of pride in you. If he has, it's because he loves you and wants to answer your prayers.

God resists the proud. Is your humiliation hindering your prayer life? Is the shame you feel causing you to hide, to excuse, to cover, to pretend? *He gives grace to the humble.* I implore you today to ask God to help you to lay all that you are and all that you feel down at the feet of a humiliated, crucified Jesus! Take up your cross of humiliation with him and follow him on the path of love and redemption. Be a captive no more to pride; and God, in his own unique way and time, will open the floodgates of grace to you.

ALL IS WELL

God is so gracious, kind, and good. He knows all about your situation today. He is not looking on with austerity and anger. The Bible tells us that he "knows our frame, and remembers that we are dust." *But healing often awaits humbling!*

Valerie's Reflections

Valerie, can you share both some positive and negative memories from your growing up years as an "MK" (missionary kid)?

Some of my favorite memories from our growing up years in the Philippines are the exciting, exotic trips my siblings and I took with our parents. Whether it was a fun-filled family vacation or an action-packed ministry trip, I loved the adventure found in traveling to new places and meeting new people. I especially loved the medical missions. There was something for everyone to do. I loved being a part of the action. I learned to give shots, but my favorite job was assisting the dentist as she pulled hundreds of teeth!

But I also remember feeling a lot of loneliness during my teenage years. I deeply missed my cousins and friends back home. I made so many friends in the Philippines, but there was a loneliness derived from culture barriers and a feeling of not quite "fitting in."

CHAPTER FIVE

Don't Bury Your Prodigal

In spite of what her natural senses told her, this grieving mother did not lay her boy in a coffin, but in Gethsemane ... on Easter morning!

There were days when the promise of our daughter's spiritual resurrection seemed dim and hopeless—a futile mirage on the horizon somewhere. Days when the weightiness of Valerie's prodigal choices tipped the scales in the direction of despair rather than hope.

During these days I (Becky) repeatedly returned to the narrative found in 2 Kings, chapter four, and the Shunammite mother's response to the death of her son. I imagined her concern as her little boy came running in from a morning spent in the field, perhaps holding his little head and crying in pain. I pondered what it must have been like as she pulled him onto her lap, perhaps thinking that he needed rest from the heat or a cool drink of water. And I could almost feel what she must have felt—her shock and grief—as he suddenly stop breathing.

There are two very different but equally destructive paths parents can take when faced with the spiritual demise of a child, and the Shunamite mother confronts them both. The first is denial.

ALL IS WELL

This is simply refusing to see the truth as it is. One thing is clear: despite this mother's broken heart, she did not deny the truth about her son's condition. She was an intelligent and discerning woman. She knew that her son was dead. There was no breath on his lips, no color in his cheeks, and no warmth in his body. There was not a fragment of evidence to offer her hope, but an abundance of facts to intensify her anguish.

How well I identified with this part of the story. There was not a shred of doubt about the fact that our daughter was spiritually dead. It was terrifying to look into eyes devoid of sight, to discern a mind comatose with regard to truth, to speak into ears tuned to lies, and to reach for a heart seemingly cold and lifeless.

There was a part of me that did not want to accept what was happening. I pondered the possibility that maybe it wasn't as bad as it seemed. *Is Valerie just passing through an abnormally tumultuous stage that many young adults pass through? Is this anxiety I am feeling unfounded?* I wondered. *As least she's not doing _____ or _____! Surely, she'll come to her senses soon!*

I am so thankful that God did not allow me to embrace these intrusive thoughts. I am confident that parents and grandparents should not take sin and rebellion lightly. We will never press through in prayer for the salvation of our kids if we do not acknowledge the seriousness of sin. The truth is that it *is* agonizing to look at the facts and accept that our son or daughter is on a path to destruction. It *is* easier at times to gloss over their stubbornness and rebellion—the two "little" sins that caused Saul to lose his kingdom[1]—and their certain consequences. It *is* difficult to bear the weight of our responsibility, to be active and proactive in praying our kids into the kingdom of God. And we will *never* persevere while living in denial.

---

1. 1 Samuel 15:23

DON'T BURY YOUR PRODIGAL

Despair is yet another dangerous response to the prodigal's condition. At times the reality of our daughter's situation would settle in, and the heaviness of it would nearly suffocate me. This had the power to nearly "shut me down." There were days when I would awaken, and only by the grace of God and sheer grit was I able to drag myself out of bed and care for my family. It was during times such as these that I longed for the burden to be lifted. Satan knew just when to assail me with thoughts such as, *She has made her choice and I have to move on. I simply can't carry the weight of this anymore. There is nothing that we can do except leave her alone and accept her condition for what it is. She is spiritually dead!*

How enticing yet deceptive this thought is, for a spirit of despair is rooted in unbelief!

As I studied the reaction of the Shunammite mother, I was so inspired by her stubborn refusal to act upon what she knew to be true about her son. Can there be anything more despairing than death? A normal, human reaction would have been for her to give way to grief, call her husband in from the field, notify her family and friends, bathe his lifeless body, prepare ointments for burial, and call for the mourners to do their thing. After all, he was dead! But her response was not natural, it was *supernatural*! She would not settle for death! Her actions speak volumes about her unshakeable faith and of her refusal to give way to despair. **She did not do the expected. Instead, she carried her lifeless boy to the prophet's bedroom, laid him on the prophet's bed, and prepared him for glorious resurrection!**

The truth in that last sentence is the heart of this book! If you miss it you've missed the message. In spite of what her natural senses told her, this grieving mother did not lay her boy in a coffin, but in Gethsemane ... on Easter morning! She ran to the prophet saying "All is well" because she knew God to be a God of miracle. "All is well" because God is a God of life, not death.

ALL IS WELL

As I read and reread this account from Scripture, the Holy Spirit illuminated the truth to my heart. I was not to give in to what I could see with my human eyes regarding the condition of our girl. I was not to entertain the thought that *maybe* the Lord could save. I was to cling to God's promises and indeed bear my daughter up on them and carry her, not to a funeral bier, but to a bed of prayer and fasting, thus preparing her for spiritual resurrection. Oh friends, let us never give up on that wayward child! Let us believe God.

Jesus said to him, "If you can believe, all things are possible to him who believes" (Mark 9:28).

For with God nothing will be impossible (Luke 1:37).

But He said, "The things which are impossible with men are possible with God" (Luke 18:27).

Now to him who is able to do exceedingly abundantly above all that we ask or think, according to the power that works in us (Ephesians 3:20).

All is well because the grace of God reaches deeper than the prodigal can fall, runs farther than the prodigal can flee, loves stronger than the prodigal can hate, and persists longer than the prodigal can resist. All is well because, *"where sin increased, grace increased all the more."*[1] **"All is well" because the light of the gospel can penetrate the deepest darkness! Believe it!**

To lay our prodigal on a bed of prayer and fasting does not mean that we cease to live or that we live in constant grief or agonizing intercession. The Lord is very aware of our humanity, of our responsibilities, of our need to live and breathe, laugh and love during this most difficult season. The act of placing our child's or

---

1. Romans 5:20

grandchild's future in the hands of a powerful and loving God, and resting in his ability to bring to life that which is dead will often bring a sense of release. It certainly did for us. Once the light of 2 Kings chapter four rose in our souls and fastened itself in our hearts, though it did not at once remove the pain or completely lift the burden, we never again contemplated burial! Valerie would live again!

Valerie's Reflections

What would you say to a parent or grandparent who has prayed for their prodigal but feels like giving up because they see no change?

I would say, "Do not give up!" Though you cannot see what is happening in your child's life, God is working. In my own story, there were many times that my sinful plans were hindered by stumbling blocks that were undoubtedly acts of God. There were many nights that I lay awake in my apartment, unable to sleep and tormented by my choices. I know now that God was lovingly pursuing me by making me miserable in my sin. This was a direct answer to the prayers of my family and friends. Those prayers brought me home.

CHAPTER SIX

The Power of Unconditional Love

The day had finally come, at long last, when the son came home. And compassion propelled this father forward. Toward his son—at a dead run, no less. Arms open wide. Love pouring forth. His heart overwhelmed.
Denise Kohlmeyer Modal

Early one morning, while our daughter was so far away from us, I (Tim) "stumbled" onto an Old Testament story which has radically transformed my understanding of unconditional love.

I had been wrestling with some of the same difficult questions many God-fearing parents in our situation have asked: *What does unconditional love look like toward our son or daughter who has willfully rejected God's authority, knowingly inflicted pain, and carelessly trampled over truth? How can we build a bridge to them without compromising God's Word? Is there ever a point at which kindness is a compromise?*

So I was meditating on this incredible story found in 1 Samuel chapters eight through twelve when the Holy Spirit opened my eyes to its application to our journey with Valerie. These chap-

ALL IS WELL

ters tell the dark story of a wayward nation—Israel—*demanding* a king, and a devoted prophet—Samuel—who, through deep, personal pain chose to act with grace. This amazing story, especially Samuel's response to painful rejection, challenged me profoundly.

In this story, as I said, Israel *demands* a king. They look at the surrounding nations, notice that they all have kings, and want one of their own. Though Samuel tries to warn Israel that a king is not God's *best* for them, they are sure they know better than God. *A king*, they think, *will give us significance, justice, and security!*[1] Ultimately, Israel's demand implied a willful rejection of God's sovereign rule over them.[2]

As I continued reading, I noticed that Israel demanded a king even though Samuel warned them of the risks.[3] "It's not going to be like you think!" he warned.

Samuel lived our story, I thought. *My warning went unheeded, too!*

"Your king is going to take from you far more than he gives. He's going to cost more than you can pay. He's going to enslave even your finest sons and daughters. He's going to steal your wealth. And there will come a day when you will weep because of your king."

This sounds familiar!

Samuel's warnings fell on deaf ears. Israel knew better, but they just had to have a king. Their disobedience was willful. Israel had become God's willfully blind, willfully unreasonable, and willfully deaf prodigal child.

I thought back to the day Valerie had demanded her king. It was a beautiful day, and we were standing by the fountain at the college she was attending. She put her arms around me and asked

---

1. 1 Kings 8:20
2. Ibid., 8:7; 10:19; 12:12
3. Ibid., 8:10-12

THE POWER OF UNCONDITIONAL LOVE

for my blessing on her relationship with a certain young man. "He's really good, Dad!" she had said. "He's not like some people have said. They don't know him like I do. *You* don't know him like I do, Dad."

"But honey," I reasoned, "I have thought and prayed about this.... As your daddy I just can't approve of a relationship I believe will hurt you.[4] Please listen to me, honey! Please trust me! You know your mom and dad only want what's best for you."

Valerie did not have ears to hear. Her eyes were blinded. She would not listen to reason because she had given herself over to wrong desire. She walked away and demanded her king, just as Israel had so long ago.

Perhaps you are feeling the frustration of dealing with a stubborn child right now. You try to reason, but your words seem to roll off them like water. It will help you to remember that sin never makes sense. Sin never responds to *reason*, because *sensual desire (flesh)* drowns it out. Sin, rooted in the heart, is not a disease that can be simply educated or reasoned away. The Bible tells us: *"The heart is deceitful above all things, and desperately wicked. Who can know it?"*[5] **The disease of sin can only be cleansed, and its power broken, through the transforming power of the gospel—** through the cleansing blood of Christ and spiritual new birth.[6]

As I continued to read this story, I began to see how relentless God's love is. Sometimes we excuse ourselves from acting with grace and kindness when the people we care about so blatantly and willfully choose wrong. Such is the nature of conditional love; but as I read on, Samuel convinced me that divine love goes farther ... much farther.

---

4. This young man has since asked for forgiveness, which we have gladly given, and desire only God's best for him!

5. Jeremiah 17:9

6. Titus 3:5-6

ALL IS WELL

This is the first part of the story that so gripped me in those hurting days: As Samuel presented Israel with their king, he said,

> *I have walked before you from my childhood to this day. Here I am. Witness against me before the LORD and before His anointed: Whose ox have I taken, or whose donkey have I taken, or whom have I cheated? Whom have I oppressed, or from whose hand have I received a bribe with which to blind my eyes? I will restore it to you.*[1]

Can you hear the grief in Samuel's voice? Does he sound a little defensive? Why is he so intent on setting the record straight? As I read these words, it suddenly occurred to me that Samuel was a wounded, hurting leader, speaking through his pain. This is a big part of what makes this story so engaging. Implied in his message is this: *"I have served, sacrificed, and loved you my entire life, and with utmost integrity, and now look how you're treating me. Am I not good enough?" This is how I feel as a dad*, I thought. Oh how I identified with Samuel. The narrative captivated me.

I knew that Samuel had been the answer to his mother's anguished prayers—prayers that God would open her womb and give her a son whom she could dedicate to God. After he was weaned, Hannah kept the vow she had made and brought her young boy to the temple, where he grew up as the servant to Eli the priest.

Samuel had grown up in the presence of the Lord and learned to respond to God's voice and speak God's truth from a tender age. Though he also grew up in the presence of moral decay and compromise, God graciously preserved his heart and his words; and Samuel became the voice of God for an entire nation.

By the time the events of chapter twelve begin to unfold, Samuel has been faithfully serving the Lord and his people for a lifetime. He had sacrificed his childhood to serve in the tabernacle,

---

1. 1 Samuel 12:2-3

THE POWER OF UNCONDITIONAL LOVE

lived through Israel's defeat at the hands of the ruthless Philistines, grieved the death of Eli and the capture of the ark of the Lord, but then became a catalyst for national revival. Samuel had given *everything* but asked for nothing, and now ... *rejection!* He took it personally. He felt it deeply, and I was feeling it with him. Since before Valerie was born until that day, I had sacrificed my life for her; but now I felt she was casting me aside. (Parents and grandparents of prodigals will understand this feeling.) I needed Samuel's advice. How will he respond? I had to know.

As I continued to meditate on this story and analyzed the choices Samuel made in the midst of his pain, I began to see a portrait of unconditional love both convicting and liberating.

First, through the account in 1 Samuel 12, Samuel taught me that unconditional love releases the pain to God and turns outward. At one point in Samuel's story he had become so focused on *Samuel* that God had to remind him, *"They have not rejected you, but they have rejected Me, that I should not reign over them."*[2] In other words, *"Don't make it about you, Samuel. This is a spiritual struggle. Israel is pushing Me away, not you!"* God was asking Samuel to turn outward rather than inward, and by doing so he became an agent of grace to this prodigal nation.

Like Samuel, dads are tempted to internalize the hurt when daughters struggle. There is a growing awareness these days among Christian dads that a close relationship with our daughters is vital to their emotional and spiritual wellbeing. So when a girl wanders away, her father often receives it, not only as a personal *rejection*, but as a personal *failure*.

In the early days of Valerie's struggle, my thoughts tormented me: *Where did I fail so badly? If I had been a better father, maybe she wouldn't have walked away. If only I had been more nurturing, more understanding, more attentive, more present.*

---

2. 1 Samuel 8:7

ALL IS WELL

In the midst of my grief I had this picture in my mind of a daddy-daughter date I took Valerie on when she was just a little girl. I remembered her pretty dress and her beaming face. It was such a special night for her ... for us. *Why didn't I take her on more dates like that? Why didn't I let her know more often how special she is to me? Why didn't I work harder at expressing my love? Am I the reason she's gone? Oh Lord, please help her know how much I love her! And, Lord, if you'll show me where I've sinned, I'll gladly humble myself! Just bring her home, Lord!* I confess that there were ways God humbled me through this pain; but as time went on, the Lord helped me realize that introspection, while *normal,* can also be debilitating. I had to trust God's grace!

In every crisis of life there are things to learn about ourselves, things to repent of, and things to surrender to God. If we have sinned against our children, or know that offenses exist between us, we *must* be the first to humble ourselves and seek reconciliation.[1] God's flow of grace to many homes has often faltered because of an unwillingness to say "I'm sorry" or accept fault. On the other hand, if we parents listen to every accusation of the Enemy, he will destroy our faith in the promises and power of the gospel. The Holy Spirit helped me see that our daughter's struggle was not because of her daddy and mommy's flaws, but because she had not fully encountered Jesus.

I know that Valerie will tell you that she grew up in a nurturing, Christ-centered home. We've always been a family that enjoys work and ministry, but we've also been a family that enjoys being together. Family play, family story-telling, and family worship and prayer have always been a regular part of our family life. We've tried to be consistent with discipline. We've tried to make Jesus and his Word preeminent and to let our children know that serving him is the greatest privilege in all the world. We've also

---

1. Matthew 5:23-24

practiced forgiveness ... a lot! But none of these things could save our daughter. Kids who grow up in the most nurturing homes still must bend their will to God's. Valerie needed a miracle that no mommy or daddy could perform.

Wallowing in our pain makes us forgetful of the gospel and forgetful of grace. This was (almost) my experience. Focusing on my hurt put me in danger of missing the real battle—the spiritual battle Satan was waging for the soul of my girl.

A second lesson I learned from Samuel is that unconditional love never seeks peace at the expense of truth. As the story in chapter twelve unfolded, I "watched" Samuel look Israel in the face and courageously declare the truth. He reminded this prodigal nation of the wonders God had worked for them in the past[2] and of his judgments when they had rebelled. And this latest rebellion—demanding a king—he called a "great wickedness"[3], and he warned them that further sin would bring further consequences. *That took guts!*

Samuel didn't sugarcoat it. He just said it like it was. Through his example, I saw that if I really love my daughter, I must never quit speaking truth. Not in a "preachy" way. Not in a forceful way. Samuel did not speak with malice or ill will but with the anointing of the Holy Spirit. This taught me that if I were to speak against sin without the power of the Holy Spirit, I might *harden* my daughter against the truth; but the presence of God in me might soften her heart and make her *receptive*. *"Lord, please help me!"* I prayed.

I saw in the narrative that God confirmed Samuel's faithful, inspired words with conviction, with terrifying displays of *power*— thunder and lightning—which caused the people great fear until they even thought they might die. Samuel's faithful words, combined with God's fearful display of power, convinced Israel of sin.[4]

---

2. 1 Samuel 12:24-25

3. Ibid., 17

4. Ibid., 18-19

ALL IS WELL

One thing Becky and I have become more and more convinced of is that parents of prodigals must never allow fear, intimidation, or even our own failures to steal our voice. Satan wants to silence us. But just as Samuel was the moral conscience and the moral compass of the nation, so we parents are of our families. Where else would Israel turn to get the truth but to Samuel? Who will tell our children the truth if we don't? God's way of preserving truth in our homes is godly parents who speak and embody the commands and principles taught in the Scriptures. Parents who persistently and wisely confront the worldly attitudes and behavior of the surrounding culture with the truth of God's Word are God's method of saving children and preserving truth in families.

These were powerful lessons I was learning that day, but a third lesson has impacted me most profoundly. **Samuel's response to Israel's painful rejection taught me that unconditional love never quits!** Love *never* stops laying down its life and offering grace to the undeserving.

As I read on in this story, I was deeply moved by Samuel's relentless commitment to serve the ones who had hurt him.

- He offers these now-repentant children hope and belonging even after all their wanderings: *"God will not forsake His people … it has pleased the Lord to make you His people."* [1]
- He offers them all the benefits of grace: *"Far be it from me that I should cease to pray for you, but I will teach you."* [2]

Often we have said to people, "You can belong, to a degree, but for mercy sakes don't ask for favors!" But Samuel would never stop working for the good of these repentant prodigals.

This hurting prophet built bridges, not walls! I thought. By God's grace I can do this with my girl.

---

1. Ibid., 22
2. Ibid. 23

THE POWER OF UNCONDITIONAL LOVE

After the people acknowledged their sin in demanding a king, Samuel (actually, God *through* Samuel) offers them a new beginning and release from perpetual guilt: *"Do not fear ... but (from now on) serve the Lord with all your heart."*[3] In other words, *"Yes, you guys have made a bad choice, a choice you can't undo now, and you will suffer the consequences for a long time to come. But today God is offering you a new start. From now on it will be as though you'd never sinned."* This is what we call "Amazing Grace!"

The implications of this truth are far-reaching. Sometimes parents just don't know what to do with children who have blown it, even *after* they've "come home." I knew that even after Valerie finally returned she'd never be able to untangle many of her decisions. Her wrong choices had carried her down the river of consequence, and she'd never be able to paddle back upstream or sail those waters over again. There were things she had lost now that she'd never get back. But by God's grace, she's never lost my love! Samuel was teaching me that I did not have to compound Valerie's sin of rebellion with my sin of neglect or indifference.

As I meditated on this, I began to see in this story the power of God's redeeming, unconditional love. Through Samuel, the Holy Spirit helped me see that love is most amazing and authentic where sin has been most willful, and that divine love can shine the brightest when people fail within our families and faith communities—people who "knew better," who "had been warned," who "wouldn't listen"! And that it is possible to be heavy on grace without being light on sin.

About the time God was teaching me about the nature of unconditional love, Christmas rolled around. Neither Becky nor I felt much like Christmas, but with Valerie's consent I picked her up on a snowy night and brought her home. That Christmas we lavished gifts on her. This was not enablement. This was not manipulation.

---

3. Ibid. 20

ALL IS WELL

This was simply love. We acted purposefully because we wanted Valerie to know that no matter the life she was living or the pain she was causing, she was still our daughter and we would never stop loving her! By God's grace I was able to say, "Valerie, Daddy wants you to know that unless you turn from the life you are living you will never find peace and will suffer consequences you cannot imagine, but I also want you to know that you are my girl and there is nothing you could ever do that would cause me to stop loving you!" I meant it!

The most powerful force in the universe is unconditional love, and the Holy Spirit wants to produce this fruit of the Spirit in each of us.

- Unconditional love for the prodigal is treating them with respect even after they have hurt us.
- Unconditional love for the prodigal will show them kindness even when they push us away.
- Unconditional love for the prodigal will keep repairing the bridges the prodigal seeks to destroy.
- Unconditional love is always looking hopefully down the road for the prodigal's return.
- Unconditional love will never say: "Get out of my life, you're no longer my child!"
- Unconditional love cannot say, "You're dead to me! I don't ever want to see your face again!"
- Unconditional love may have to ask the prodigal to leave our home but will never let them leave our hearts.
- Unconditional love will not protect the prodigal from the painful consequences of their decisions, but it can never reject them or push them out of our lives.

THE POWER OF UNCONDITIONAL LOVE

Unconditional love will melt the frozen heart. I have seen it! Unconditional love has incredible power because it flows from the heart of God.

Beloved, let us love one another, for love is of God; and everyone who loves is born of God and knows God (1 John 4:7).

A Prayer of the Prodigal's Father

Father, I'm hurting ... really hurting! I'm being tempted right now to nurse my wounds—to feel sorry for myself. I feel myself becoming self-focused. I'm tempted to personalize and internalize the failures of my child. But Father, may your powerful, unconditional love for me, in me, and through me, rise above the pain and produce in me a heart of grace for _____. Help me, Lord, to learn to love like you do, and to always speak the truth, but with wisdom, love, and grace. May your love be a powerful tide to pull them back to the shore. In Jesus' name. Amen.

Valerie's Reflections

What part did unconditional love have on your return "home"? Can you give an example?

One thing I always knew, even in my rebellion, was that my parents and family were the ones who truly loved me. Most of the time I didn't feel lovable at all, and I didn't know how they could. When I first moved away, I didn't have a vehicle and walked almost everywhere. I walked through feet of snow to work during the winter and sometimes, when I didn't have a ride, back to my apartment in the dark.

I remember when my dad reached out to me about buying a car from them. He offered to bring the car to me and told me that I could pay him a little each month. I was shocked that my parents would want to help me even when I knew they didn't agree with the way I was living. There were many other times I felt their unconditional love—a surprise birthday party shortly after I ran away, making a five hour round trip on Christmas Eve to pick me up, and always welcoming me back home with open arms. These things softened my heart. Had I been treated as a black sheep and shunned because of the choices I was making, I firmly believe it would have completely turned me away. I was able to tangibly feel God's unconditional love for me through my family during those months.

As a mother myself now, I have often thought of how my parents must have felt during my time away from home. It still saddens me even though we have a wonderful relationship today. Reading about the struggles they went through because of *me* has not been easy. But I am so thankful for their faithfulness.

Thanks, Mom and Dad, for your unconditional love. No matter how you felt, you never stopped praying for me or reaching out to me. At one point you drove hours to see me and talk to me in person. I can still see the pain on your faces and the desperation in your voices as you pleaded with me to return. You didn't make it easy for me to get away.

If you had washed your hands of me, and concluded that I was an adult who could make her own decisions, things would have turned out much differently. I felt the walls I had built up crumbling that day as I tangibly felt your love—a love that would do whatever it took to get me back to God. I knew you weren't going to let go until your prayers were answered!

CHAPTER SEVEN

The Waiting

For how long this father waited is uncertain. Scripture doesn't say. But he waited. Every day. Expectantly. Prayerfully. Hopefully. May God grant parents of prodigals that kind of Spirit-filled patience.
Denise Kohlmeyer Modal

The days of worry and wondering about Valerie's well-being dragged painfully on into weeks and then months. I (Becky) found myself living for the relief I felt each time she sent a text, and agonized when I heard nothing for extended periods of time. She lived only a few hours away, but we knew nothing about her living conditions. *Is she safe?* We wondered. *What kind of friends is she hanging out with?* We knew that she was very naive and very beautiful.

I had had many conversations during her growing up years, conversations that had come out of hearing various stories on the news. You know, those tragic stories of teenage girls disappearing, never to be found. I tried to talk candidly with her about the dangers of being in the wrong place at the wrong time and with the wrong people. I must admit that during these days I was desperately afraid for her safety. We prayed earnestly that God would place a hedge of protection around her despite her foolishness.

ALL IS WELL

I found this place of "in between"—the middle place between the prayers and the answer—to be unbearable. It was not natural for me to be still and trust. This place of *waiting*, when I would have preferred to be *doing*, fixing, and answering my own prayers, threatened to be my undoing. I longed for peace and rest and reprieve from the inner turmoil.

I realized that this is not God's plan for his children—that I was not to allow Satan to terrorize me. After all, I was a child of the Creator. Surely he could give me peace and hope in the midst of the unknown.

I discovered that the key to this peace was to saturate myself with God's Word. I would awaken each day and delve hungrily into the Scriptures, immersing my heart and mind in the truths I found. I allowed God's voice to quiet my fears, and I learned to praise him in advance for what I knew he would surely bring to pass. I wrote out promises and commands of Scripture and their application to our situation.

The words found in Psalm 37:7, *"Rest in the Lord and wait patiently for Him,"* took on new and powerful meaning. During these days, the last thing I wanted to do was to rest and wait. Although I know they are not, these words sounded passive to me. Passivity and my self-sufficient pride were not compatible. I was hardly a patient person. I wanted to act! I wanted to do something to fix this situation and bring our daughter to her senses. Waiting patiently and resting were not my initial "go to" strategy.

Matthew Henry's notes on this verse were so applicable to me. In his commentary, he states that to "wait" means to "*compose ourselves by believing in God. Not discompose ourselves by what we see in the world.*" Mr. Henry is also right when he states: "*A fretful, discontented spirit lies open to many temptations—and those that indulge it are in danger of doing evil.*" This was true for me. My temptations were to be short and impatient with my husband and young children. When I caved to worry, I was overwhelmed and

THE WAITING

inefficient. I found it nearly impossible to rise above the feelings of negativity and stress. Those temptations—anger, stress, impatience—opened the door to sin in my life.

Exercising patience while waiting for the promise is for our good. For when we do, we are not shaken by what we see but are steadied by quiet expectation, knowing that he will in his time answer our prayer.

Lettie Cowman included the following powerful excerpt on "waiting" in her devotional, *Streams in the Desert:*

> **Patience takes away worry**—he said he would come, and his promise is equal to his presence.
>
> **Patience takes away weeping**—why feel sad and despondent? He knows your need better than you do, and his purpose in waiting is to bring more glory out of it all.
>
> **Patience takes away self-works**—the work he desires is that you believe, and when you believe, you may know that all is well.[1]

I needed to allow these truths to penetrate my mind in the days of waiting.

Because God is kind and compassionate to his weak children, he also heard my desperate cries for his presence when I stumbled along the path of resting and waiting.

One day I awakened with such heaviness in my spirit. A spirit of despair was threatening to overwhelm me. My legs felt leaden, my heart was filled with anxiety, and I could scarcely pray. I sent an SOS to heaven, pleading with God to give me a supernatural glimpse of himself and to assure me that he was indeed looking out for Valerie.

I opened up my email just two hours later and found messages from two people—people whom I barely knew and had certainly

---

1. Lettie Cowman, *Streams in the Desert,* February 21

never discussed our daughter's needs with. They both wanted to let me know that they had been fasting and praying for Valerie! They had felt prompted by the Holy Spirit to do so. I wept and praised God for hearing my prayer and for his undeniable answer to it.

There was a day when I struggled throughout the day with feelings of doubt about Valerie. Sadly, I had given an ear to the constant murmurings of the Enemy. I was overwhelmed with thoughts that perhaps she would never give her life to God, that our relationship would never be restored, and that she would be destroyed spiritually, emotionally, and physically.

It was a dreary, rainy day, and my choice to mull over these negative thoughts had left me short and ill-tempered with my little girls. I was devoid of joy that bleak afternoon. Later that evening, the rain had eased up and the girls had gone outside (probably to escape their gloomy mom). Suddenly the door burst open and Samantha ran into the house shouting, "Mommy, Mommy, you've got to come outside and see this!" Her excitement drew me out into the driveway where looking up I saw one of the most brilliant rainbows I had ever seen. It seemed to encompass the sky, beginning at one end of the horizon and falling into the earth at the other. I stood there on the wet pavement gazing into the heavens when, to my amazement, a second rainbow appeared! It was stunning and splendorous and awe-inspiring! Tears filled my eyes, and I heard the voice of God gently reminding me, *"Becky, I always keep my promises."*

I went back into the house that evening praising God that his Word is fully trustworthy and that he would come through for our daughter—that he would rescue her. I felt so loved and cared for. It seemed that he put on this glorious display just to remind me of who he is and what kind of character he possesses.

Perhaps you are currently in a time of waiting. Perhaps your situation is bleak and you see no deliverance on the horizon. May-

THE WAITING

be you have been waiting for years for your answer and are tempted to believe that perhaps your loved one is beyond the reach of God's redemptive arm. Dear friend, during your season of waiting, God longs to pour out his deepest care upon you. He wants you to be surrounded by his loving presence in ways that can only be experienced when all other comfort is absent.

I implore you to focus on the kind of God for whom you are waiting. According to Scripture, he is:

The God who performs miracles (Psalms 77:14, NIV)

The God whose "*arm is not too short to save; nor his ear too dull to hear*" (Isaiah 59:1, NIV)

The God who promised to "*Pour out my spirit upon your offspring*" (Isaiah 44:3b, NIV)

The God who "*Gives strength to the weary*" (Isaiah 40:29, NIV)

The God in whom we put our hope, for "*with the Lord is unfailing love and with him is full redemption*" (Psalm 130:7, NIV).

These and many other promises are underlined and both tear and coffee stained in my Bible as I read them again and again, gaining strength and hope for the wait.

And you can too. Allow God's Word to carry you through the waiting.

Read it!
Live in it!
Write it down!
Meditate on it!
Believe it!
Pray it back to God!

God's Word is powerful and living and able to destroy the lies Satan may be whispering in your ear right now.

ALL IS WELL

Let the peace of God carry you through this day—not tomorrow, or next week, or next month—just today!

Andrew Murray reminds us: "He knows when we are spiritually ready to receive the blessing to our profit and his glory.... Be assured that if God waits longer than you could wish, it is only to make the blessing doubly precious."

Valerie's Reflections

Valerie, what goes through your mind when you reflect on this chapter?

I am so humbled when I read about all the people who prayed and interceded for me during those months I was running. My faith has been strengthened even more just hearing the memories my parents have of different ones reaching out to them during that difficult time.

There were days I was sure that most people had written me off. I know now that it was the Devil trying to convince me I had already gone too far and messed up too much. I cannot thank my parents and their friends and the rest of my family enough for not giving up!

CHAPTER EIGHT

*Praying **For** and **Against** the Prodigal*

Go on your way, and God bless you, for it is not possible that the son of these tears should be lost.
A bishop, reassuring Monica, the mother of Augustine, that God would answer her prayers for her son.

We'll never pray effectively *for* a willfully wayward child until we learn to pray both *for* and *against* them!

Our God is a mover of mountains[1] and a destroyer of strongholds. A mountain or stronghold certainly includes any immovable, moral obstacle to the advancement of his good, righteous kingdom in the hearts of our children. Prodigals need faith-filled dads and moms who believe that *prayer,* not *flesh,* is the weapon God uses to win the toughest battles.

> *For though we walk in the flesh, we are not waging war according to the flesh. For the weapons of our warfare are not of the flesh but have divine power to destroy strongholds (2 Corinthians 10:3-4, ESV).*

---

1. Mark 11:23

ALL IS WELL

By the spiritual weapon of *prayer, divine power* is released to tear down obstacles in the way of God's kingdom in the hearts of our children. But one of the most important lessons God taught me (Tim) through this prodigal journey was that I could not wield the *weapons of the Spirit* with the *arm of flesh*! The "arm of flesh" is an expression the Bible uses to express our best *human* efforts.[1] The arm of flesh will always weaken one's prayers.

My arm of flesh was anger. Valerie's stubborn demand for things I knew would wound her made me angry. Really angry! *How can she not see the foolishness of her ways?* I thought. *These eighteen years we have prayed for her, loved her, instructed her, and encouraged her. How can she so easily dismiss and reject us? Can't she see what she's doing? Why won't she listen?* And then she would stand in front of me with a look of stubborn defiance (this is hard to write) and blatantly disobey and disrespect us, and I would boil over at the "insanity" of it all!

In the months leading up to Valerie leaving home I would often try to reason with her. When I sensed she wasn't listening, I would raise my voice and hope that the force of my words and the passion of my heart for her would somehow break through her pride. But neither anger nor passion prevailed. Does it ever?

One day, not long after Valerie left home, the Lord opened my eyes to the truth of these words and their application to our struggle:

> *Know this, my beloved brothers: let every person be quick to hear, slow to speak, slow to anger; for the anger of man does not produce the righteousness of God (James 1:19-20, ESV).*

Those words, *"for the anger of man does not produce ... righteousness"* hit me between the eyes. *I have been trying to produce righteousness my own way—with the arm of flesh*—I thought. *I have*

---

1. 2 Chronicles 32:8,

PRAYING FOR AND AGAINST THE PRODIGAL

been trying to pry my daughter's eyes open through anger. I have turned up the volume in hopes that the sound of my voice would awaken her. But, according to God, this is futile! Through his Word, the Holy Spirit reminded me that my anger would never produce the righteousness Valerie so desperately needed. Only he could produce that in her through his Holy Spirit. After this I began to rely more perfectly on prayer.

I do not want to be misunderstood here. The Word of God is also a powerful weapon of our warfare[2], and fathers and mothers *must* speak truth to their children. We must constantly confront the lies of the human heart and the lies of the surrounding culture with the truth of God's Word—taught clearly, respectfully, and gracefully. But there is an end of words. A time will come in the life of many children that the Word already sown must be left for the Spirit to germinate. We must discern when this time comes.

While there is an end of words, there is never an end of prayer. And here are a few truths we have found most encouraging regarding prayer for the prodigal:

First, God hears the pleadings of the prodigal's parents. There is a powerful Old Testament account where God was ready to destroy the nation of Israel because of their rebellion, but Moses *"pleaded with the Lord"* to spare them[3]. He *begged* the Lord to spare their lives.

> *And the Lord said to Moses, "I have seen this people, and indeed it is a stiff-necked people! Now therefore, let Me alone, that My wrath may burn hot against them and I may consume them. And I will make you a great nation."*

With these words the future of thousands of families and an entire prodigal nation hung in the balance. God was not faking.

---

2. Ephesians 6:17

3. Exodus 32:11

ALL IS WELL

This was no empty threat. This nation was deserving of nothing but complete annihilation. Just like you. Just like me. Just like our prodigal child.

The next sentence is one of the most powerful in all of Scripture: *"Then Moses pleaded with the Lord his God...."*[1] This *pleading* moved the will of a sovereign God. *"So the Lord relented from the harm which He said He would do to His people"*[2] (32:14). Pleading prayer matters! Our pleadings shape the future of our children.

By his pleading Moses became the protective hedge on the precipice which kept many from falling to their death. If he hadn't been there, if he had neglected his call, if he had chosen indifference, if he had not prayed, a rebellious nation would have tumbled to their death.

> *Therefore he said he would destroy them—had not Moses, his chosen one, stood in the breach before him, to turn away his wrath from destroying them (Psalm 106:23, ESV).*

This should both encourage and challenge us. What a powerful weapon prayer is! And what a tremendous responsibility we have to stand in the gap for that child who is headed toward destruction.

Second, the strongholds in the hearts of that prodigal may only be broken at personal cost, through a season of fasting and prayer. This rightly-motivated self-sacrifice deepens our humility (dependence on God), fills us with the Spirit of Jesus, strengthens our faith, and moves mountains.

Moses became so intense and serious about the salvation of God's people that he spoke words almost unthinkable: *"Yet now, if You will forgive their sin–but if not, I pray, blot me out of Your book*

---

1. Exodus 32:11
2. Ibid, 32:14

PRAYING FOR AND AGAINST THE PRODIGAL

which You have written."[3] Bible scholars tell us that when Moses spoke these words, he was expressing his willingness to be erased from God's Book of Life[4] if only his life could be traded for the lives of his people! Such was his deeply-felt longing for their salvation. Just like Jesus, his burden became so great that he became willing to lay down his life for the sake of his people. This is the kind of love many Christian parents understand.

One of the ways the Lord taught Becky and me to offer ourselves to God for the sake of Valerie was through fasting and prayer. The practice of fasting was a common practice in Scripture when God's people found themselves engaged in intense battles and when the stakes were high. Jesus taught that fasting would be a normal part of discipleship.[5] And throughout the history of the church, fasting has been a normal practice.

- Fasting humbles us.

The psalmist said, *"But as for me, when they were sick, my clothing was sackcloth; I humbled my soul with fasting."*[6]

Abstaining from physical food reminds the soul of its utter need for, and dependence upon, God. Biblical, Christ-centered fasting is a testimony to God and to our own soul: *God, I'm hungry for you. Holy Spirit, I need you more than food, more than physical or material blessings, more than anything in this world!*

- Fasting strengthens our faith for the tearing down of strongholds.

Matthew tells us of a time that the disciples found themselves powerless to cast an evil spirit out of a young man. They wondered

---

3. Ibid., 32:32
4. Daniel 12:1
5. Luke 5:35
6. Psalm 35:13

ALL IS WELL

why. Jesus made it clear in the story that unbelief was the root problem and that unbelief could only be overcome through prayer and fasting.[1]

Jesus indicates that there is a relationship between fasting and faith. Prayer with fasting strengthens faith in God and therefore increases our effectiveness in prayer. When we are fighting for our sons and daughters, we must remember that we are engaged in spiritual battle which may not be won without self-sacrifice.

Let's be clear: You and I don't naturally have it within us to love this deeply and passionately, but the Holy Spirit within us can love like this. Are you willing to be anguished *with him* over the soul of your son or daughter? Are you willing to care this much, *by his grace*? Ask him to help you. Ask him to give you a sight of eternity and the hell your wayward son or daughter is tumbling towards. Humble yourself with fasting, and ask Jesus to give you a heart that yearns so much for their salvation that you become willing to give up sleep and food for a season of intercession.

Be careful here.

We are aware that words like this can quickly lead parents of prodigals into spiritual bondage. Bondage is praying, not as sons and daughters in union with Christ, but as servants driven by slavish bondage—praying as though everything depends on us rather than grace. This season of our lives taught me that I have no love of my own. On my own I cannot care deeply about my loved ones. On my own I am selfish and unwilling to sacrifice. On my own I have no passion for the lost. All the love and concern and passion is in the heart of Jesus, and he produces it in me by his Spirit as I depend on him.[2]

One of my former instructors in Bible college warned Becky and me of the danger of *graceless* praying for Valerie. He and his

---

1. Matthew 17:23
2. John 15:4ff

PRAYING FOR AND AGAINST THE PRODIGAL

wife had learned this years before while praying earnestly for the salvation of a loved one. He warned us that while fervent prayer and fasting are vital, there must come a time in our intercession when faith takes hold of God's promises and finds rest; that after we have pled with God and waited before him there would come a time when he would give us a glimpse of the answer. The Bible says it this way: *"Now faith is the assurance of things hoped for, the conviction of things not seen."*[3] When faith breaks through, we become convinced that the King of the universe has said *"Yes!"* in heaven and will soon grant it on earth.

I will never forget the night that faith for Valerie's salvation finally broke through. She was still running, still seeking happiness in all the wrong places. Becky and I were praying with our younger four before sending them off to bed. As we did consistently, we included Valerie in our prayer; but this time I sensed something unusual. We became aware of the presence of God, and freedom was given to us to plead for her like never before. I knew that the Holy Spirit was pleading through us, that our Father was hearing us, and that somehow he was causing our prayers to reach his throne.

Later that night Becky and I were sleeping soundly when I suddenly awoke. A profound peace filled the room, and these words were powerfully impressed upon my mind: "The battle is not over but the war is won." I knew this was the gracious pronouncement of the Holy Spirit to my heart that our months of praying had been heard and that redemption was on the way. The awareness of God's presence and the assurance to the heart of this father was indescribable.

After this our prayers became less intense. We entered a season of peaceful prayer and praise where we continued to pray but without the heavy burden. We knew that Valerie was on God's hook and he was reeling her in!

---

3. Hebrews 11:1, ESV

ALL IS WELL

One more thing we'd like to say about effective prayer for the prodigal is that we must be willing to pray *against* them!
In some ways, this was one of the hardest things we had to do. To pray *against* Valerie felt almost like a betrayal, only it wasn't. We came to see it as the most loving prayer we could pray. Dr. Allan Brown, one of my Bible professors in college, taught us to pray for our unsaved loved one something like this:

> *Father, draw them to Jesus.[1] Grant them a heart of repentance. Create a hunger and thirst in them for you. Oh God, as long as they are happy in sin, they will not sense their need of you. Therefore, cause the pleasures of sin to turn to ashes and dust in their mouth. Hedge them in to your will and your way."*[2]

To pray *against* the prodigal is to pray for their conviction of sin. We daily prayed the promise of Jesus in John 16: *"And when (the Holy Spirit) is come, He will convict the world of sin, and of righteousness, and of judgment."* We asked God to make Valerie aware of her sin and to make her tremble before him. We asked him to make her profoundly aware of eternity and of the terror of spending an eternity separated from his presence.

To pray *against* the prodigal is to pray for their unhappiness. We regularly prayed that Valerie would find no joy, no peace, and no comfort in the pleasures of sin. We asked the Lord to take away the sweet taste of sin and turn it into bitterness in her mouth.

To pray against the prodigal is to pray that God would bring people across their path to speak truth into their lives and to remind them of him. This we also prayed regularly, and God answered.

As the months passed, we came to the point in our prayers where we prayed, *"Oh God, deliver our daughter at any cost.... Please don't let her die in her sin."*

---

1. John 6:44
2. Hosea 2:8-9

PRAYING FOR AND AGAINST THE PRODIGAL

Becky and I know that some who read this will think we are too strong. We understand. But when we remembered warnings like this from Jesus regarding hell and judgment and eternity, we believed every word:

> *For what profit is it to a man if he gains the whole world, and loses his own soul? Or what will a man give in exchange for his soul? (Matthew 16:26, NKJV).*

A little temporary discomfort is nothing compared to an eternity in hell.

One day, not long after Valerie had come "home," a woman confided in Becky. Her heart was broken over a son and a daughter who had walked away from God. After listening to this story for some time, Becky told this mother how we had prayed *against* Valerie and how the Lord had answered our prayers. "Oh, I could never do that," she said. "I can't stand to see my children unhappy."

Many parents feel this way, because the truth is that when our children suffer, we suffer too. So it's not easy. But love understands that pain is often what God uses to turn the prodigal's heart toward home.

Let's be parents who stand in the gap for our kids. Let's take up the powerful weapon of prayer and see the breakthroughs God works in the hearts of our children.

Dear Father, I pray right now for every parent and grandparent whose heart is heavy for their prodigal. Teach us to pray ... fervently ... faithfully. Remind us, Lord, of the power of this weapon to tear down every argument and break through any and every stronghold. In Jesus name. Amen!

Valerie's Reflections

Looking back, were there moments in your prodigal journey when you believe the prayers of others restrained you from certain wrong choices and protected you from greater harm?

A naive, sheltered twenty-year-old girl living on her own for the first time is not a good mix. I shudder when I think of some of the situations I put myself in during the nine months I was running from the Lord. I am so very thankful for the constant prayers of my family and friends during those months. One particular time I was in search of a new job when I received a phone call from a foreign number telling me they were looking for someone to be a nanny for their children. I was signed up on a website that had all my information as well as a picture displayed on my profile. Looking back, the whole thing was very suspicious and too good to be true. They gave me an address and time for an interview. Upon arrival, I quickly realized something was amiss. The house was abandoned and in a back part of town with no one around. I never got out of my car, even though I thought about it. After only a couple of minutes, I drove away realizing I had been scammed. I'll never know what would have, or could have, happened to me had I gone up to the door of that house; but I firmly believe the prayers of my family and friends kept something terrible from happening that day.

CHAPTER NINE

The Grace of Christian Community

Therefore, confess your sins to one another and pray for one another, that you may be healed. The prayer of a righteous person has great power as it is working.
James 5:16

I (Tim) stood in the lobby of a mechanic shop near our home waiting for an oil change. My thoughts were never far from Valerie. The heaviness of heart, the constant gnawing in the stomach: these are the dogged companions of a prodigal's parent, even in the midst of ordinary routines. My cell phone rang. I was surprised to hear the voice of a professor from my college days, Rev. Edsel Trouten, on the other end of the line. I had not heard from him in years; and I knew he lived in Idaho, some two thousand miles from Cincinnati. "Hello, Tim, how is Valerie doing?" he began, characteristically cutting out the small talk. "Our prayer group has been praying for her, and for you and Becky, and I want to give them an update tonight when we meet."

I was amazed. Everyone who knows Edsel Trouten knows he is a man who believes in the power of prayer. I was deeply touched by his love. I hadn't spoken to my former professor in years, and I had no idea that the Lord had put Valerie on his heart. I cried (yes, this happened a lot during those days). I shared our burden. He encouraged me, and before he hung up he prayed for us. I will never forget the blessing his call and his prayer meant to Becky and me.

Calls like this, and sometimes texts, happened several times during the nine months that Valerie was running. I'll bet we can remember most, if not all of them! One morning when our hearts were especially heavy, a friend of mine from across town sent a most encouraging text. He said that he didn't know a lot about what we were going through but that he had received a strong ability to pray for Valerie that morning. This text, and others, made us aware that the Holy Spirit was at work and that he was bringing about our daughter's redemption through the body of Christ.

Redemption is a team effort! At least it should be.

In some of the most desperate times of our lives, our family has found refuge in our Christian community. Through the cancer diagnosis of our newborn son, Jesse, we learned how precious the family of God truly is. As missionaries experiencing times of loneliness, fear, sickness, and spiritual warfare, it was our faith community that helped pull us through. And we could not have made it through this experience with a prodigal daughter without God's family.

We were created for community. We were created in the image of the triune God with a capacity and yearning to know and to be known. *We were created for fellowship.* We were created for *deep and meaningful relationships*. We were redeemed, not just for our own sake, but *for the sake of each other*:

- Bear with one another (Ephesians 4:2)
- Forgive one another (Colossians 3:13)
- Comfort one another (1 Thessalonians 4:18)

THE GRACE OF CHRISTIAN COMMUNITY

- Edify one another (1 Thessalonians 5:11)
- Confess your trespasses to one another (James 5:16)
- Pray for one another (James 5:16)
- Have compassion for one another (1 Peter 3:8)
- Have fellowship with one another (1 John 1:7)

These are just a few of the "one another" passages in the New Testament. Christianity is about spiritual family! We are commanded to live interdependent, connected lives with other believers for the good of all.

Vulnerability is a key to healing

True community depends on one thing that terrifies us—a *childlike vulnerability*. The kind of vulnerability that says, *"We have nothing to hide! No reputation to protect! We need help! We can't do this on our own! We're weak!"* Community is a gift of grace; but until we are willing to become vulnerable before that community, we may not get to experience the fullness of this grace.

Yes, all of you be submissive to one another, and be clothed with humility.[1]

When our hearts are breaking, and when we feel embarrassed, we tend to go into hiding. But hiding plays right into Satan's hands. Parents and grandparents who are tempted to isolate themselves when children and grandchildren struggle should be aware of how isolation can weaken them, making them more vulnerable to discouragement. Like a lion that harasses a herd until one member is tempted away from the protection of the "community," so Satan wants to isolate God's children. Once alone, we are easier prey. But authentic, grace-filled, Christian community is a refuge.

---

1. 1 Peter 5:5

ALL IS WELL

In the beginning of our prodigal struggle, the least natural thing in the world for us was to open up and share our heartbreak. To speak *out loud* the things that were in our hearts was unspeakably painful ... for a lot of reasons. We ourselves could scarcely believe the circumstances we were in, and so to give voice to them felt like ripping bandages open to expose our ugly wounds. But the Lord helped us see that to *not* open up would keep us from the healing we so desperately needed.

Vulnerability within community brings grace.

I (Becky) am so thankful that God enabled us to approach godly people and to share our situation. Instead of judgment, we found compassion; instead of blame, we found understanding; and instead of indifference, we found people who gladly opened their hearts and entered into intercessory prayer with us.

I'll never forget the night my sister called and said that during a prayer meeting she attended, the Holy Spirit had so filled their hearts with fervent intercession for Valerie that people were crying out to God for her deliverance. She said it sounded like a labor and delivery room! We hardly knew how to respond to such testimonies. We were astounded that people cared so much.

We also sought counsel. We asked questions of leaders whom we trusted and listened to their advice. Once we reached out to a godly couple and shared our doubts about remaining in the ministry while Valerie was running. We felt completely overwhelmed and unworthy of spiritual leadership. We wondered, *since our own child has gone astray, shouldn't we just bow out of Christian ministry until she returns?*

This seasoned pastor and wife had also walked this prodigal road with a son and knew exactly what we were going through. They, too, had struggled with thoughts of leaving the ministry, and the wife especially felt that she should give up all positions of ministry in the church. She told us how one day in prayer God assured her, *"Daughter, if you will take care of the things that matter to me, then I'll take care of the things that matter to you."* She did, and God did! And today their son is serving God as a pastor. We treasured insights like this from believers we trusted.

I cannot over-emphasize how important our immediate and extended family was during these months as well. But opening up to them was also a sacrifice. We found it humbling to tell our story with those closest to us. It had a way of bringing the reality of our situation into clear focus. It was painful to see the disappointment on the faces of those who'd loved and invested in Valerie from childhood, especially my sisters because we are so close. But the support and healing we discovered in opening up was worth the risk!

Tim and I firmly believed that we had to lay down our pride and fear. We had to resist the temptation to just ignore reality and hope it would go away. We needed to face into the stormy wind. We had to accept the place we were in. We could not sugar-coat sin. We had to lay our situation before God and our spiritual community and believe that the Lord would bless our vulnerability.

The value of community cannot be overstated. To know that there were others carrying this burden with us gave us the physical, spiritual, and emotional strength we needed to get through each day. With four other children at home to care for, we had to get up each morning, "wash" our faces, take fresh hold of the promises of God, and walk confidently through another day. We could not have done this alone.

God was so faithful along the way to give us tiny glimpses of his power and affirmations of his behind-the-scenes work to bring about a mighty answer.

In the last chapter Tim told of how he awoke at 3:00 a.m. one morning with a powerful promise for Valerie being impressed upon his heart: *"The battle is not over, but the war is won!"* I'll never forget how he awakened me and through joyful tears shared what God had just spoken to him. *"Becky,"* he said, *"we need to praise God right now for what I know he is going to do."* We laid in the bed and thanked God for hearing and answering our prayers. We thanked him in advance for rescuing Valerie. Lying there in the darkness we were filled with confidence that it would come to pass.

What Tim did not share was what happened the next afternoon. I received a phone call from my sister Julia. *"Becky, what was going on with Valerie last night?"* she asked. Before I could answer, she continued, *"In the middle of the night, Dave* (Julia's husband and Tim's brother) *woke me up. It was around 3:00 a.m. He said, 'Julia, the Lord has given me such a burden to pray for Valerie that I can't carry it alone. Please ... I need you to help me pray for her.' We prayed together for a while until the Lord gave us peace."*

What an awesome God! And what grace there is in the church—the body of Christ! We felt incredibly loved and cared for, knowing that while we were sleeping others were "watching" in prayer; while we were resting, others were breaking through. And God had sent a heavenly Messenger to whisper the news of victory in Tim's ear!

If you are where we were, please do not miss the grace that God wants to pour into your life through your Christian community. I challenge you toward childlike vulnerability. I encourage you to humble yourself before a faithful brother or sister in Christ. You don't have to use a megaphone to announce your sufferings to the world. You shouldn't hang your dirty laundry in plain view of every curious eye. But you *must* ask the Lord to give you a circle of friends and family to help you bear this burden.

Valerie's Reflections

What influence have your Christian friends and extended family had on your return and your walk with the Lord?

I was a bridesmaid in two of my closest cousins' weddings during the nine months I was "running." They both married Christian men and were surrounded by supportive family and friends on their special days. I shed many tears thinking I might never get that chance. I have been so blessed to be surrounded by Christian family and friends my whole life. The example I have seen all around me from birth to adulthood is something I don't take for granted! Watching my peers serve Jesus and make right choices has had a huge impact on my own life decisions. Now I get to live side by side with close cousins and friends who are striving to raise children for Jesus and to build strong Christian marriages, just as I am. I am so grateful!

CHAPTER TEN

He Must Win the Battle

I never had the experience of looking for God. It was the other way round; he was the hunter and I was the deer. He stalked me ... took unerring aim and fired.
C. S. Lewis

It was mid-June and we were beginning our summer touring schedule—a very busy time of year in which we visit summer camps and represent the foreign mission arm of our denomination. As you have read, it had been a difficult year for us. Valerie had been away from us for about nine months. With all that we were experiencing with her, life was stressful! My (Becky) heart just wasn't in traveling, meeting people, smiling, talking about God's power and the wonderful things that he was doing in other parts of the world. I was in a place where I desperately needed God's power to be at work in our family—our daughter—and in my own heart. Tim and I both still struggled with a sense of unworthiness, too. Were we even qualified to lead this ministry, to represent God's work in other countries? We sincerely wondered. Who were we to be up front talking and encouraging others to trust God, to support missions, and to offer themselves completely to him for the sake of the world's unreached when we had failed to disciple our own daughter?

ALL IS WELL

On a Wednesday night of family Bible camp, I wasn't doing well. I was hardly a stellar example of a faith-filled, ardent missionary! Tim and I sat in the front on the right side of the building. The place was packed out, and there were additional chairs set up in the back to accommodate the crowd.

As we stood to sing, I did my best to tune out the plethora of worrisome thoughts running through my mind and to focus on worship. It wasn't easy. We hadn't heard a word from our daughter for a couple of weeks and my mind had been fraught with anxiety, wondering where she was and how she was doing. But the presence of God inhabiting the praises of his people began to carry our spirits upward.

The atmosphere was filled with beautiful music and a spirit of worship. I focused on the screen in front of me and the hymn that we were singing—the timeless hymn penned by Martin Luther centuries ago: "A mighty fortress is our God." As these beautiful words of truth rang out, God began to speak powerfully to both Tim and me:

> Did we in our own strength confide,
> Our striving would be losing,
> Were not the right man on our side,
> The man of God's own choosing.
> Dost ask who that may be?
> Christ Jesus, it is he.
> Lord Sabaoth, his name,
> From age to age the same,
> And he must win the battle.

And he must win the battle! It was as if we had never heard those words before. The truth about God's almighty "battle winning" power became real to us. This was not *our* battle! This was *Lord Sabaoth's* battle—the Lord of Hosts! *We* could not win it, but *he* surely could! I felt God speak to me, and Tim sensed him speaking to his heart as well. Our weary hearts were strengthened as faith began to rise. Although Tim kept singing, I stopped, sat down, and began interceding for Valerie. This was something different. I prayed not out of fear, sorrow, or desperation, but with boldness, confidence, and joy. My prayers were faith-filled. I truly believed that what I was praying was coming to pass. I knew that in that moment God was working in our daughter's heart. I didn't know how, or where, or what was happening; but I knew that as I prayed on that night there was a battle somewhere being waged for the heart of our girl and that God was winning.

I awakened early the next morning and noticed that we had received a text from Valerie at around 3:00 a.m. "Mom, I need you!" she wrote. I was unable to reach her right away, but later that afternoon Tim received a text: "Dad, where are you? I need you and mom! Wherever you are, I am coming to you." We sent the address and waited, feeling overjoyed, a bit apprehensive, not knowing what to expect, but believing that this was the beginning of our miracle.

Valerie arrived several hours later—a tearful and broken girl. She sat on the bed in our small, cramped camp room and shared the events of the previous twenty four hours: that she and a friend had "stumbled" into a Christian youth camp the previous evening; that she had heard a powerful message spoken from the Gospels about "leaving your nets and following Jesus"; that God had gripped her heart with longing and conviction of her sin; that she hadn't had the courage to go forward but had lain awake until 5:00 a.m. in utter brokenness over her situation.

I was overcome by the truth of God's sovereignty as she shared with us. It had been no coincidence that we had been called to prayer during a worship service the previous evening. God had surely been busy *"winning the battle"* and had let us in on the action, although we had no way of knowing how things were playing out in Valerie's life. This gave us such assurance of his power at work, but we knew that the Enemy might not let go easily. We chose not to say too much. God was obviously at work and we didn't want to interfere. We prayed with her and took her home with us that night.

The truth of these words, "And he must win the battle," persisted in my mind and heart for the next nine days, for it was as if we were engaged in hand to hand combat with Satan over the life of Valerie.

She was home—but restless. Tim and I each sensed a wariness in her—an unsettled spirit. We were thrilled to have her home, but I couldn't help but note the troubled expression she wore.

On Tuesday morning, Tim awakened early and peered into Valerie's bedroom. Her bed was empty. He went to the front door and looked out into the driveway. Her car was not there. He returned to the bedroom. His face was pale and his voice weak. "Becky, she is gone," he whispered.

I moved quickly, throwing on some clothes, all the while telling Tim, "This is Satan. He is out to destroy the work of God in her life." This was an all-out war! We weren't about to let him win. I felt that we should go after her. Tim agreed.

Some of you who are reading may strongly disagree with us. It's okay. We know that this is not always the right response. Honestly, I surprised myself that morning. I'm not one to act quickly or rashly. But for some reason, we were compelled to jump in the car and head to where we assumed she was going. We were right.

A few hours later, we sat in our car a few doors down from Valerie's apartment. We weren't even sure of what to do. We certainly couldn't force her to return home, nor did we want to. We only wanted her to know how much we loved her and that we were willing to support her in making the right decision. We sent her a text. We told her that we were just a block away, that we were not there to coerce her, but that we needed her to look us in the

HE MUST WIN THE BATTLE

face and tell us that this was what she wanted. Within minutes she joined us.

We sat together at a little outdoor table. With tears streaming down her face, Valerie told us that she couldn't remain in her hopeless situation; that she wanted to do what was right; that she wanted to leave her sin behind. We stayed with her that day and helped her to do some difficult things. We helped her pack up everything she owned, returned library books, and then with two cars packed, we headed for home.

Satan doesn't let go easily. He will fight to the death for the hearts and minds of our children. Once he has pulled them down the prodigal road, the path home may sometimes be a process. For our daughter, the desire to follow God was there; prayers were constraining her to return to her faith; and the Holy Spirit was convicting her of sin. He had planted a hunger for righteousness within her, but her Enemy was throwing every obstruction imaginable in her way to keep her from following through.

There was such a spirit of struggle in our home that week. It was exhausting. On Tuesday evening, Valerie called me down to her room. "Mom," she said with sadness in her voice, "I think I'm leaving again. I'm going back." There was a look of utter despair on her face, as if she was resigned to the fact that she could not withstand the pressure—that this was her destiny—she had already done so much, and gone so far, there was really no hope in trying to do what was right.

It broke my heart, but we didn't argue or try to change her mind. *He must win the battle!* Tim and I simply asked if we could lay hands on her and pray for her. She said "yes." We prayed a simple prayer, asking God to defeat Satan's plans for Valerie and that he would give her an abundant life in Jesus. Words fail to describe the nearly tangible spirit of darkness that was in the room as we prayed. I went to bed that night knowing that we had no ability to fight against this foe. The truth of those words, *"And he must win the battle,"* was so real to Tim and me.

The following day was much the same. We spent the evening with family. We kept the conversation light and fun. It was good, but Valerie was pensive and quiet. There was an underlying struggle that was as real as the very air we were breathing.

We awakened on Thursday morning to find that Valerie had packed up and left sometime during the night. Although not totally unexpected, I still felt as if the air had been sucked out of my world!

Tim and I were *beyond* physically and spiritually exhausted. We had been living in a constant state of desperate prayer for days. We had been face to face with the Prince of Darkness. He had been assaulting our home. He was waging an all-out war to steal from us the peace of God, the promises of God, the protection of God, and most of all, the life of our girl.

And he must win the battle. It was true, and, once again undeniably clear to both of us. We were done! There was not another thing for us to do. We were too exhausted to worry, to fear, or to even pray. I remember crying aloud to God that morning, *"Lord, this is your fight! We are finished! If you do not rescue our daughter, then no one can! This is all on you, and we know that you are up for it!"*

The peace of God pervaded the darkness over our home! It was sweet and pure. There was such release that Tim and I left the house and went for lunch.

I was not aware that morning that several of Valerie's cousins who had been praying for her throughout her prodigal journey had decided to begin a serious fast. These young people—mostly teenagers—began "blowing up" one another's phones with text messages declaring that they would never let her go. They decided to intercede for the salvation of their cousin. It was as if we were tag-teaming our prayers. Tim and I were spent and weary. God released us to rest and called upon these "kids" to pick up the prayer torch and march on! They fasted and prayed into the weekend.

Saturday afternoon, we packed a picnic lunch and went to a beautiful lake near our home. It was a typical sweltering July afternoon in Ohio. The kids and Tim spent the day in the water while I enjoyed a thick novel on the sandy beach. It felt good to rest and read something far removed from the trauma of the week.

I received a text from Val late in the afternoon: "Mom, I'm on my way to Virginia. I've really left my life behind, and I'm never going back." I read the text to Tim. *Is this real?* we wondered

Why is it that when our prayers are finally answered we are sometimes slow to believe it? I remember thinking, *"Yeah right! You'll get to Charleston and decide to turn right around!"* I'm ashamed of this, but grateful that God understands our hearts!

Valerie arrived sometime in the early morning hours of Sunday. After only a few hours of sleep, she got up and attended the Eastlake Community Church with her cousins. My brother Troy is the senior pastor.

Troy didn't know that Valerie was in the service. He had not seen her come in. But God did, and he was winning the battle! The evangelistic service had been planned for months. God's presence was in the building in a powerful way as person after person walked to the platform, sharing written testimonies displayed on large cardboard posters. Testimonies such as: *"I was an adulterer, but Jesus forgave me,"* *"I was in bondage to _____, but Jesus set me free,"* *"I was defeated by _____, but now I have victory in Jesus!"* One after another, messages of hope and deliverance were read by the audience. God was speaking to our girl. My brother stood and gave an invitation to anyone who desired new life in Christ. He looked up and saw Valerie nearly running to the front of the church! She was the very first person to respond that Sunday morning. This was her moment! At that altar on July 3rd, 2011, Valerie's new life began!

ALL IS WELL

Listen to this powerful thought found in *Streams in the Dessert*:

Many a Christian's prayer is hindered by Satan, but you need not fear **when your prayer and faith pile up, for after a while, they will be like a flood and will not only sweep the answer through but will also bring some new accompanying blessing.**"[1]

I had come across this quote the very week of Valerie's return. I had taken the time to record it in my journal, believing as we struggled through those tumultuous days, the weight of prayers that had been piled up over Valerie would someday be poured out by the Holy Spirit and carry her home. We still rejoice in this mighty outpouring of grace!

Let this encourage you. Your situation is different than ours. Your journey will have twists and turns and detours that we haven't encountered. Every family's story is unique, and the endings will not all look the same. God will work in your life and in the life of your son or daughter in his own unique way. But he *will* work! Not one humble prayer of faith will be ignored by our heavenly Father. Not one restless night will pass unnoticed. Not one whispered prayer will go unheard. Not one desperate plea will be wasted. Your love and faith and prayers are piling up! Lord Sabaoth is gathering his army and *he must win the battle!* Believe it! In him, through him, and for his glory ... *All is Well!*

Celebration!

November 25, 2011 was an unforgettable day. Family and friends gathered in Virginia for Valerie's baptism. There were nearly fifty of us there. We worshiped. Valerie testified of her faith in the Lord Jesus, of her commitment to follow him, and of her grat-

---

1. Lettie Cowman, *Streams in the Desert*, May 16, emphasis added

HE MUST WIN THE BATTLE

itude for those who had loved and prayed her home. Becky and her sisters sang a beautiful song of praise and thanksgiving. There were more testimonies. And then Troy and I (Tim) immersed Valerie under the water. She came up smiling! It was a beautiful, powerful, joy-filled moment, a true celebration of a prodigal's return, a true celebration of a loving, gracious Redeemer.

> *"Bring out the best robe and put it on him, and put a ring on his hand and sandals on his feet. And bring the fatted calf here and kill it, and let us eat and be merry; for this my son was dead and is alive again; he was lost and is found." And they began to be merry (Luke 15:22-24).*

Valerie's Reflections

Valerie, can you reflect on the events leading to your return "home"?

The days and weeks leading up to my return home were completely miserable for me. I honestly don't think I stood a chance against the prayers of God's people on my behalf. A couple weeks before my return home for good, I attended a Christian youth camp just to hang out with some friends. The last night I was there, Pastor Mark Cravens was the speaker. He preached about "leaving your nets to follow Jesus." I remember feeling such conviction over my sin. It wasn't fun anymore. I wanted to run home as fast as I could! I couldn't sleep that night, and sat up talking to a good Christian friend of mine before driving back to my apartment the next day. As I walked into the place where I was working to start my shift that evening, it seemed everything had changed. I didn't want to be there. Everything looked different, and I felt a heaviness I had never experienced before. Now I am sure that those were the physical answers to the prayers being prayed for me. This was the start of my bumpy road home!

What was going through your mind when you left home again in the middle of the night after you had returned?

The journey home, after going down the road of complete rebellion, was one of the most difficult and tumultuous times of my life. The choices I had made during my time away left me emotionally and physically wrapped up in the wrong things. These things had me in complete turmoil. As soon as I arrived home the first time, doubts began to creep into my mind. I didn't believe that after all I had done I could come back and be made whole again. I didn't think I could ever heal. I felt as if the choices I had made were irrevocable.

Can you share your testimony of what God did for you that Sunday morning at Eastlake?

The third time I left my small apartment I traveled through the night and arrived at my grandparents in Virginia in the early hours of Sunday morning. I slept a couple hours and then went to church. It was Friend Day and there were powerful testimonies and a gospel concert. At the close of the service, we sang the song "Mighty to Save." As we sang about a Savior who can move mountains and who is the author of salvation, I was reminded of what I always had known deep down in my heart. God loved me. He had pursued me for so long. Even though I had turned my back on him, he still wanted me today. There was an invitation, and I knew today was the day. Today was the day I would turn away from the sin of my old life and completely give myself and my stubborn pride over to the Lord. I'm so thankful for that day and the people that God placed in my life during that time.

Were you ever tempted to return to your old life?

Even though the biggest battle of my heart was won that Sunday at church, I faced many challenges in my heart and life in the days following. The Devil fought me hard in the early days. He told me I would never amount to anything, that I had blown my chances of a good life, that no Christian man would ever want me after the things I had done. When these intrusive thoughts would come to my mind, Satan would tempt me to turn back to my old life. I know the prayers of my family and friends were still covering me and holding me back from making another bad decision. I'm so thankful for the truth of the Word of God and the support of my family.

AFTERWORD

A Final Message from Valerie

When my parents first approached me about writing *All Is Well,* I felt a little bit of fear. It felt intimidating to be part of the subject matter of a book. Weren't those kinds of people the ones who have finally arrived and whose lives are perfect? I know that this is not true, but it was a bit daunting to launch out and share some of our story with all of you.

I am in a different season of life now. These days, I'm in knee deep (and some days over my head) with the joys and challenges of motherhood. My days consist of supporting my husband, taking care of our home, dealing with the terrible two's, pregnancy nausea, and enjoying my four-year-old (who thinks she is sixteen). My struggles are different now, and God is always stretching and shaping me.

As I think back upon the events that you have read, I realize that this book is not about me, it's about God's amazing grace and redemption. It tells of a God who didn't stop chasing me even when I was running fast and far away from him. My parents have been sending these chapters for me to read, and I have enjoyed being still and reflecting back on these tumultuous events in all our lives. It has been emotional at times, but good. I don't ever want to forget the miracle God has brought about in my heart and life.

Now more than ever I know how amazing it is to experience

just what God can do when we finally surrender our hearts and lives completely to him.

How well I remember that long drive through the evening of July 2 and on into the early morning hours of July 3. I was confused, lost, and brokenhearted. It was as if a power beyond myself was driving me, both literally and figuratively, through the night, far away from the life I had been living, and pushing me mile after mile towards home. I know now that it was the urgent intercessory prayers of my parents and family that powered me on. I didn't have the strength to do it on my own. I will never be able to adequately thank them for not giving up on me.

That Sunday morning was the day that I was brought to my knees in brokenness and repentance. Looking back on the days, weeks, and months following my move to Virginia, God's hand is evident in every detail. God so graciously provided a wonderful job and career path for me. My Uncle Troy and Aunt Janel took me into their home and provided a safe and loving place for me to heal. I had no idea that I was also living just down the street from my future husband, whom I met a few months later.

Brent is a solid, stable Christian man. My family quickly made an effort to get to know him and could see what a wonderful man he was. It was evident that he was the man for me. What began as a friendship quickly blossomed into love, and in less than two years, on June 15, 2013, we were married. It was one of the happiest days of my life. We have since welcomed two healthy girls into our family, and our first son will be joining us in a few months. God is so gracious and kind. He lovingly took the mess I had created, the mistakes I had made, redeemed them all, and saved my life! His redemptive work continues in my life even now. I am so undeserving!

My hope and prayer for this book is that it will fall into the hands of those who need it now. I know that what my parents have written will help many parents of wandering children, even those

AFTERWORD

who spent many years away from God. I also pray that there will be young people who are currently "on the fence" or beginning to rebel and stray who will read this account and see my perspective from the other side. Your parents and those surrounding you are wise; they are not trying to destroy you with their counsel. Being determined to have your own way is very costly, and regrets are painful. Most importantly, true happiness and contentment lies in a life surrendered fully to Jesus. God's way is the best and only way to *truly* live!

Friend, we welcome a conversation regarding the content of this book! If you would like to share how *All Is Well* has impacted you, or if you have questions or comments related to the content of this book, please feel free to write to Tim and Becky at timandbeckykeep@gmail.com. They would love to hear from you!

Tim and Becky Keep enjoy sharing their stories of God's faithfulness. To request Tim and/or Becky to speak for your conference or special event, please contact them at timandbeckykeep@gmail.com, or on Facebook at TimandBeckyKeep.